DEEP

DEEP

Frog and Amy Orr-Ewing

MILTON KEYNES ● COLORADO SPRINGS ● HYDERABAD

Contents

To the congregations of All Saints, Peckham and
St. Aldates, Oxford

Deep Church

God is powerfully at work around the world in churches of all shapes and sizes. We spent eight years in Oxford, serving in a big, long-established, city-centre church with a thriving ministry to university students. There we experienced God's miraculous power, as He brought salvation and healing to many. We believed that God would bind up the broken-hearted and that He has purposes for the poor and needy. But what would it really be like to move out of our comfort zone and live somewhere completely different, without the infrastructure of a successful church around us?

These thoughts raced around in our heads in 2003, as we contemplated moving from Oxford to London. We knew that God is faithful and is not confined by material constraints – but knowing something in your mind is not the same as living and experiencing it. At 27, Frog was the youngest incumbent in the Church of England when he was appointed Vicar of All Saints, Peckham. We were on our own, leading a church in one of the most needy areas in our nation.

It was August 2004. Our church was in the middle of the largest mission we had ever attempted. It was part of a London-wide initiative called Soulinthecity in which hundreds of churches did events, concerts and evangelism across their respective local areas. We were preparing for an evening youth event with a great band, an outside concert on the church site and a guest speaker. Helping us were over a hundred young people from other parts of the United Kingdom and teams of friends from America.

Things had been hotting up, and we had heard stories of a chase down the main street in Peckham very near our church the previous afternoon, in which local teenagers had been targeted. So we were praying hard for the youth event to go smoothly. At 5 p.m. a message got through to us in the prayer room: 'We need the vicar. There are youths clinging to the gates, demanding to speak to you and claiming sanctuary!' (Unusually, we had closed the church gates to allow for the set-up of PA equipment and chairs.)

I (Frog) rushed outside to find about nine young people ranging from 11 to 16 years old, asking to be let into the church site, and scared for their lives, having been chased the day before by people with machetes and nail-filled planks of wood. Two gangs had called in reinforcements and it was all scheduled to kick off at 6.30 p.m. on Blenheim Grove – just outside the church as people were due to arrive at our evangelistic event. I naturally granted sanctuary and told the people in the prayer room to get busy. I informed the police, who came quickly and stood at the gates – and so the proposed gang fight was diffused.

The group of young people stayed in all evening. Gill, our speaker, who at that stage knew nothing of these goings on, spoke powerfully about Jesus, the Good Shepherd, who lies down across the gate and provides safety and sanctuary for the sheep, protecting them from predators. All those young people who had sought refuge in the physical church site took the opportunity that evening to pray with team members, and many of them remain known to us today. At times of crisis people are quick to seek sanctuary.

In 2007 our community of Peckham in south-east London was in the news again for all the wrong reasons. With gun crime on the up and violence rife, a teenage boy was shot to death in his bed whilst he slept at night – an apparent victim of mistaken identity, and one of three young people killed in four days in separate incidents. This shooting happened just down the road from our home – less than a five-minute walk away. Amidst these bleak headlines, living in Peckham there are people from at least 300 distinct cultures from all around the world. Here the rich and the well-educated live side by side with the deprived and the badly educated. And right at the heart of things there are growing churches and many people committed to making the Peckham of tomorrow different from the Peckham of today. Our church is one of these. We have been in this community since 1867. Agencies may come and go, individuals may pass through, but the church is here to stay – a constant presence in the community.

Many of the stories we tell in this book are things we have seen and experienced along our journey of Christian leadership, although occasionally we will change the names to protect anonymity. We don't apologise for the use of so many stories of lives changed by Christ in a book about 'Deep Church'. We have theological convictions about a real God who actually acts in his world, and if our theology is correct, it will be born out in real-life situations. For us, Deep Church must transcend individual congregations, and it is not merely a set of ideas. Rather, it is lived out day to day in local churches in all sorts of different areas.

We believe that our experience of London can serve as a parable, for it is not unlike the state of the church in the West – vibrant and alive, with a window on the world, filled with signs of hope, rich with limitless potential and possibilities, and yet somehow also discouraged and despairing, with a seeming inability to grasp the opportunities when they arise, and beset with the problems of ethics and lifestyle issues. In the face of all this, advancing as a missionary church and wrestling with the intensity of the spiritual battle can be exhausting, and so some choose to take refuge in hoping for nothing (an unbiblical option), and others begin to harbour secret, deep doubts (an unspiritual option). This disillusionment is the true root of the so-called 'post-Evangelical' and 'post-Charismatic' movements of recent years. We have no doubt that the disillusionment is real, but we also feel that it is unnecessary. As the theologian Ian Stackhouse writes:

> the delay of revival success has encouraged a general weariness. To be sure, there have been claims of revival, but nothing matching the numerical expectations of the early pioneers of renewal has yet taken place, with the resulting pathology that arises from a 'hope deferred'.[1]

We are discovering on this journey that only bold, certain and spiritually alive Christianity has the answer to a context like this. As a missionary congregation in the twenty-first century, we need to be more deeply Evangelical and evangelistic than ever, deeply and truly reliant on the power of the Holy Spirit, deeply engaged with our culture and the needs of our community, deeply realistic about our limitations and temptations, and deeply convinced of our faith in the face of all other worldviews and alternatives. We have been blessed in seeing Jesus move and work so wonderfully in our streets, schools and estates in the last few years – it's impossible not to get excited about it!

Our central conviction, then, in response to the disillusionment we find amongst so many, is that Christians should not have to choose between essential elements of New Testament Christianity. We shouldn't have to choose between social engagement and great biblical teaching with fearless exposition. We shouldn't have to decide between high standards of discipleship and contemporary justice issues. We shouldn't have to opt for mission at home instead of abroad. We need not neglect inspiring worship in order to be sensitive to outsiders, or neglect the mind in favour of encouraging the flourishing of the gifts of the Holy Spirit. In the face of the current reticence *about* and questioning *of* the Evangelical faith, we should not abandon or water down the amazing message of salvation that we have. Rather, we must recapture what is most important, whilst keeping our expectations bold, courageous and *scripturally* realistic (and therefore high!). Now is not the time to draw back from expecting signs and wonders and experiencing the fullness of the Spirit; now is not the time to forget our heritage as missionary-minded Evangelical Christians; now is not the time to dampen our passion in worship of Jesus; now is not the time to retreat from a vision of transforming our society.

So when we were given the opportunity of delivering a series of talks at the New Wine Conference in the summer of 2007, we choose the title 'Deep Church', in part to allow us to articulate some of what God has been teaching us and challenging us about on the journey we have shared with our local church in the last five years. Under this heading we covered the issues of 'Deep Passion', 'Deep Mind', 'Deep Character', being 'Deeply Physical' and being 'Deeply Immersed' in the community.

The phrase 'Deep Church' is not our own at all. It was coined by C. S. Lewis and has more recently been picked up by some of the UK's best contemporary theologians. But it has struck a chord with us as we live to see the Kingdom of God coming in our church, community, city and nation. More than anything, 'Deep Church' is about restoring the heart of our faith within a rapidly changing and demanding culture, without lurching from one new methodology or technique to another, and rescuing today's church from unnecessary disillusionment and avoidable spiritual *ennui* (boredom), and instead embracing Christ and His Kingdom with everything that we have and all that we are.

This is part of a movement which is occurring at ground level in churches all over the place. Andrew Walker comments:

> There is a wind of change blowing through the evangelical world, carrying on its wings a new watchword, which is neither 'renewal' nor 'revival', but 'retrieval'. The fact of its newness, however, should not deceive us into thinking that it is the title of yet another transitory technique of pragmatism borne on the breezes of religious enthusiasm. Paradoxically, what is new about this retrieval is that it is a quest for something old, and its modus operandi is not a technique but a turning back.[2]

So retrieval is vital but not at the expense of what is fresh. We continue to need also a daily reliance on the renewing power of the Holy Spirit. It is appropriate to nurture in our prayers a longing for revival, but we also need to be reformers. Reformation is the discernment process of authentic spirituality, which keeps our message sharp and relevant, testing and approving what is biblical and valid in our ever-changing and challenging culture – it is our process of scriptural self-critique. We shouldn't have to choose between reformation, renewal, retrieval or revival. In Haggai 1 we see a picture of all four in tandem.

Reformation

The post-exile population of Jerusalem had attempted to rebuild the temple several years earlier, but had run out of steam, and had concentrated instead on what they thought they could handle – reworking their own homes. But this materialism and property upgrade had not led to satisfaction or even a good harvest. In many respects they were disillusioned and frustrated, and struggling spiritually and financially.

> Then the word of the LORD came through the prophet Haggai: 'Is it a time for you yourselves to be living in your panelled houses, while this house remains a ruin?' Now this is what the LORD Almighty says: 'Give careful thought to your ways. You have planted much, but have harvested little. You eat, but never have enough. You drink, but never have your fill. You put on clothes, but are not warm. You earn wages, only to put them in a purse with holes in it.' This is what the LORD Almighty says: 'Give careful thought to your ways. Go up into the mountains and bring down timber and build the house, so that I may take pleasure in it and be honoured,' says the LORD.
>
> Haggai 1:3–8

Their priorities and goals had slipped from their high-minded ideals of previous years, and perhaps despair had set in. Into that context God spoke and called them afresh to the task which had once inspired them. The temple that Haggai was charged with motivating his generation to rebuild was a ruin. Rubbish and rubble filled the place, the stones had been shattered, the walls had tumbled in, the wooden gates had decayed and the precious fixtures and fittings were nowhere to be found. Before the rebuilding could go ahead, the rubbish needed to be cleared away, and this is the task of reformation. Charles Spurgeon makes the point clearly:

> When Paul began to build for God, and the apostles went forth as wise master-builders there lay before them in towering heaps the old Jewish rubbish, hard to remove, heavy to bear away. . . . A master excavator was Martin Luther; how grandly he laid bare the glorious foundation of justification by faith alone! An equally grand worker at this grand enterprise was John Calvin, who laid open long stretches of the ancient foundations of the covenant of grace.[3]

Retrieval

Despite the fact that the ancient site of the temple was filled with rubble, some of the enormous stones on site could be re-used and worked into the fabric of the new structure. So long as they were solid and usable, they could be hugely valuable. For example, large segments of St Peter's Basilica in Rome are made from the dressed stones of the Coliseum, re-used by Italian builders hundreds of years after the Romans had constructed the stadium. It is the same reason that makes reclamation yards so popular today, as people build with Victorian bricks and old cast-iron radiators. Similarly, we do not need to start Christian doctrine from scratch in every generation: we have the immovable rock and foundation of Christ himself, upon whom all Christian thought depends; we have the stones of Scripture, reliable, tested and trustworthy; also we have firm and dependable Christian doctrine, often summed up in the creeds or great confessions of faith. The author Dorothy L. Sayers provocatively wrote:

> We are constantly assured that the churches are empty because preachers insist too much upon doctrine – 'dull dogma', as people call it. The fact is the precise opposite. It is the neglect of dogma that leads to dullness. The Christian faith is the most exciting drama that ever staggered the imagination of man – and the dogma is the drama. That dogma is summarized quite clearly in the creeds of the Church, and if we think it dull it is because we either have never really read those amazing documents, or have recited them so often and so mechanically as to have lost all sense of their meaning.[4]

Renewal

God told the people of Jerusalem to go up into the mountains and fell fresh wood for the important building project. The new temple couldn't be constructed by working with reclaimed bricks alone. Fresh and firm timber was needed, not only for the scaffolding, but also for the panelling and the roof-beams. Today's church cannot rely on a reworked faith alone – it cannot be reliant on yesterday's moves of God, assigning the power of the Holy Spirit in the life of the believer to doctrinal formulations or the times of the apostles. To do so is to relegate to history something that Scripture expects as a present reality, and to rob this generation of believers of the gifts and the seal of the Spirit which are rightfully theirs. In the

English church this reappraisal and recapturing of the personal infilling of the Holy Spirit as normative for the believer is often called 'renewal'.

Revival

A fourth element in the call to rebuild is the spiritual expectation of revival – an understanding that the purpose of a rebuilt temple is the honour and pleasure of God, or literally that it might be filled with glory. The same promise comes clearly also in the next chapter: '"I will shake all the nations; and they will come with the wealth of all nations, and I will fill this house with glory," says the Lord of hosts' (Hag. 2:7 NASB). Prayer for revival is characterised by a high expectation that people from all backgrounds and nationalities will come to faith in God, and that there will be a tangible sense of His presence or glory. In the middle of a sermon on revival, Charles Spurgeon broke into prayer: 'Oh that at this moment he would open the windows of heaven, and send us a flood of grace, till the tops of our loftiest expectations should be covered.'[5]

Some rubbish needed to be cleared – reformation. Some stones could be retained as good material – retrieval. But new wood was needed from the mountains – renewal. And a promise of acceptance, salvation and glory remained – revival. These four emphases form a backdrop to a Deep Church, whose expectations are high, whose passion is real, whose scope is wide and whose faith, experience, thinking, character and impact are all deep, enduring and effective.

The call of Deep Church, though, is not just for theologians, church leaders, congregations and small groups collectively; it is also about each individual Christian experiencing and knowing that Jesus rescues from the depths and changes them deeply.

Danny (not his real name) was brought up in care, he went to one of our local schools, and was dangerously depressed. He came to school late and left early, wanting to avoid as many other students as possible. The bullying had already led to an incident when acid had been thrown on him in a science lesson, and there were concerns from the staff that he might take his own life. The head teacher said to one of our congregation members involved in schools work there, 'If your God can do something for him, then I'll be really interested.'

A year or so later, after involvement in an open club and the Christian Union, and having spent time with a youth mentor from the congregation, the boy became a Christian. He was filled with a new confidence, was baptised, began writing Christian songs and even ran an Alpha course within the school. He went away with a group from our church to a Christian camp. He had saved up to buy sweets and snacks whilst away, but instead he spent his money on gospels and tracts to take back to school so that he could share with others what Christ had done in his life. A personal encounter with Jesus has turned his life around from hopelessness and despair, and made him part of the hope-filled future for our community. We are still working in the school, and the fact that this one young man's life has been transformed through Jesus has made a significant impact on the staff.

Our approach in writing this book is to take six dimensions and apply them to five different themes. By taking *worship, the word, history, action, mission* and *leadership*, and applying them to our Christian *passion, mind, character, body* and *community*, we are trying to take a holistic approach to becoming Deep Church. It is our prayer that as you read this, the glory of Jesus and His Kingdom will come through rather than the successes of particular individuals or congregations. After all, the people in the stories we mention only want to point to Christ.

Chapter 1

Deep Passion (1)

The phrase 'Deep Church' is taken from C.S. Lewis, who, when asked about his churchmanship, replied that his preference was neither for high church nor for low church, but rather for deep church.[1] This has resonated strongly with us as we have come to the realisation, through conversation with friends, our pastoral work and in a number of books we've been reading, that there is a dangerous cynicism that can come into the Christian life. A shallow, paltry kind of Christianity is all too common. Disillusionment ensues. It may be that a church has prayed for a revival which didn't come, and the leader, who had been convinced that it would come, just completely ignores the fact that it didn't, and moves on to the next 'new' thing. After several years of this, we can end up with a kind of boredom. We don't want to say that we're bored, because we know that as Christians we're not meant to be bored, so we never really talk about it. A great contrast with this *ennui* or disillusionment can be seen at the end of Philippians. This serves as a challenge and an encouragement to us that our walk with God is not meant to be like that. Paul is in prison and he's been fighting the fight and walking the walk of the Christian life for many years, but he is still able to say, in chapter 3:

I press on to take hold of that for which Christ Jesus took hold of me. Brothers, I don't consider myself yet to have taken hold of it, but one thing I do: Forgetting what is behind and straining towards what is ahead, I press on towards the goal to win the prize for which God has called me heavenward in Christ Jesus.

At the end of his life and ministry, Paul was still absolutely passionate, on fire, committed, excited about his future on this earth as well as his heavenly calling. We can sometimes lose that passion.

This interplay between passion for God and a struggling, lukewarm faith is something which has been important in my (Frog's) life. My parents went their separate ways when I was about 3 and my sister was 18 months old. I grew up in a loving context where my mum went to church occasionally and my father went about two or three times a year. They say that 'C. of E.' stands for 'Christmas and Easter', and that definition was pretty accurate for our nominally Church of England family. I would say that growing up with this contact with Christianity and the church meant that I definitely knew that there was a God.

I went away to boarding-school when I was 9, and the school I went to was fairly traditional, with compulsory chapel every morning. One of the things that I struggled with as a young boy was a sense of being moved from pillar to post – my parents moved house 14 times between them before I turned 14. My sister and I were parcelled around from one parent to the other and experienced the weird transaction that occurs where you're taken down to the bottom of the drive and your other parent's car comes to pick you up. My sister and I were both also forgotten at school when everybody else was collected at the end of a term. I'll be honest and say that

I wasn't the least complicated person in my school – in fact, I dread to think of all the files they must have had on me! I was pretty disruptive.

Years went on, and I went off to the next boarding-school. I attended Bible studies and the Christian Union there. I understood the gospel and had begun to follow Christ, but I was pretty badly bullied and was sent to hospital a couple of times. By the time I was about 14, I had actually reached moments of suicidal thoughts. I was sharing a room with a guy, who's still a friend of mine now, and he tells me that I used to talk about just 'ending it all, life is so miserable – I'm going to end it all.' But in the midst of this year I was invited to go away to a house-party (a mini Christian conference). I had an opportunity to go along to the 'Holy Spirit' seminar, where they just talked very simply about who the Holy Spirit is.

Now, the term before, I remember sitting in my school chapel again and looking up and seeing the chaplain in all of his regalia. A very, very clear thought passed through my mind. It went like this: 'What an appalling job that must be! How strange and how boring!' And I thought, 'Well, if Christianity is true – if it really is true that God is real, that He died on the cross to save us from our sins, that He was resurrected, and if all of the things that are in Scripture are real – then it should change the world and I should give my entire life to this cause.'

And then I looked at this guy and thought, 'He doesn't look as if that is what he is into at all. He doesn't seem to be living as if this is the world-changing, life-changing message from the God of the universe to us, His people, to set the church on fire.' And I thought, 'There's a mismatch here between the kind of Christianity I'm living in and what it's like in the Bible.'

I was sitting in this Holy Spirit seminar about six months later, and things began to make sense. He was the missing ingredient. The Holy Spirit is more than just the last bit at the end of the Creed where it says, 'I believe in the Father, the Son and the Holy Spirit.' That was all the look-in he'd got at school chapel every single day for seven years.

Somebody said, 'Would you like to be prayed for?' and I said 'Yes, I'd love to be prayed for.' And as I sat in that room, with just a few of us gathered around, somebody began to pray for me. I was absolutely overwhelmed by the presence, power and love of God. It started to flood through my very body, like electricity surging through my veins. I realised that God loved me. As I realised this, I heard him say in my mind: 'I want you to be alive. I want you to be alive.' Now, that may not sound like a revelation, but if you've had moments of wondering whether life is worth living, knowing that God loves you and wants you alive is a big deal. I started to cry.

Somebody prayed for me to receive the gift of tongues, which I then received there on the floor. And as I wept, suddenly joy entered my heart. The Scriptures say, 'The joy of the Lord is your strength.' In my place of despair and darkness and brokenness, wondering whether there was a purpose for my life, whether there was security in the world, the joy of the Lord, a supernatural joy, entered my heart and my soul. I then started to laugh, and I was laughing so hard that tears were streaming down my face, mingling with the previous tears of sadness.

That day I wrote in my diary the fateful words: 'I wonder if God wants me to be a vicar.' I was 14.

After this experience, the teenage hormones kicked in and I had a very bumpy ride. I was living a kind of a dual Christian existence – my heart, soul and vision of the future had Jesus firmly at the centre, and yet my lifestyle was not matching up to that. I had a vibrant spirituality, I loved worship music, I attended Bible studies and invited friends to the Christian Union, but I was also a socialite and wanted to be the life and soul of the party. Then in 1994, after I had lived this dual life for about five years, one of my friends, who was working in the bookshop at Holy Trinity, Brompton, told me I had to come and experience what God was doing in that church. So I went there every Sunday for about six weeks. In the meetings there, everybody around me was laughing and seemed to be feeling the fullness of the Holy Spirit, and I just felt completely miserable. Having failed God routinely for so long, having not lived the Christian life, I just sobbed under a conviction of sin, knowing that there was such as distance between me and Him. At the end of that summer, the Holy Spirit really started to work in my life and it felt like God had said to me, 'OK, you've been weeping and you've said sorry now for six weeks continually for having failed to live the life.' And then He said to me: 'I love you, I accept you.' And here was the crunch for me: 'I don't just want you to be alive – I've also got a plan and a purpose for your life.' I mulled that over. 'I want to use you, I don't just want you to be a good boy.' A dichotomy had built up between my spiritual existence and my 'real life'. I had wondered whether God had anything to say to me in my physical existence, but there's nothing like being shaken violently by the Holy Spirit for about seven days to make you realise that He has power over matter, as well as over spirit! A deep work of God happened in me.

Worship

We live in a society today where people perceive religious passion as something inherently dangerous and risky; something which is to be avoided at all costs. G.K. Chesterton comments:

> A common hesitation in our day touching the use of extreme convictions is a sort of notion that extreme convictions, specially upon cosmic matters, have been responsible in the past for the thing which is called bigotry. But a very small amount of direct experience will dissipate this view. In real life the people who are most bigoted are the people who have no convictions at all.[2]

In our church we're seeing people in their twenties and teenagers come to Christ, and suddenly their parents are terrified that their child has become a religious nutter. Being Church of England can help to diffuse this panic, as the C. of E. is hardly known for radical passion. But this fear is a reality largely because of the rise of Islam, where people who have a passion for God and a passion for what they believe is His word are committing acts of violence in the name of that God.

I (Amy) vividly remember 11 September 2001. I'm sure we can all remember exactly where we were. I went home to Frog and we sat in front of the TV, watching the replay of the aeroplanes as they went into the Twin Towers. We had done some study and writing on Islam and we'd been involved in evangelism to Muslims, and so we wondered if this act of violence would wake up people in the West to the fact that Islam can be interpreted in an extremist way.

A few days later I gave a talk about the Christian faith, and at the end, as I often do, I answered some questions from the audience. The first question was:

'Isn't what you are preaching as Christians *dangerous*? Isn't it *dangerous* to believe in your Holy Book and to be passionate about your God? Because look what happens when you take religion too seriously! Isn't it dangerous to be a fundamentalist, whether that be a Muslim or a Christian Evangelical? Isn't passion a dangerous thing?'

I was stunned – absolutely stunned. I had never been asked this question before, but I would say that now this question comes up nine times out of every ten that I speak.

I was even more stunned later to hear that a high-level meeting had happened at Oxford University to talk about religious tolerance, and in that meeting, al-Muhajiroun, a fundamentalist Islamic organisation, was compared with All Souls, Langham Place, that 'bastion of dangerous fundamentalism' in London, as if the two were in some way equivalent.

We live in a society where passion is seen as something dangerous, but of course, this need not be the case. Being passionate about something is only dangerous if the object of your passion inspires violence. If the object and subject of our passion commands compassion and peace, the outcome will be completely different. The Bible teaches that God wants us to be passionate for Him – passionate in a good way. He wants us to be passionately on fire for Him.

What does it mean to passionately worship God? The Psalms help us with this. When you open the Psalms, it's overwhelming to see how often the psalmist writes things such as: 'Praise the Lord', 'Give thanks to the Lord', 'Come, let us sing to the Lord', 'Sing to the Lord a new song for what he has done', 'It is good to praise the Lord and make music to him', 'I will sing to the Lord'. In a church context, where we've grown up as Evangelical or Charismatic Christians, we may have become very familiar with the various patterns of worship. However, there is an act of the will involved in worship. Passionate worship involves choosing to sing, choosing to declare, and entering into worship with our whole hearts.

There may be various blockages to doing this, such as dreary music, overly 'folksy' music, or things being repeated one hundred thousand million times. However, the Bible says that entering into praise and worship of God is a choice, and that obedience to God means that we choose to do that exuberantly, whatever our style and however old we are.

My favourite hymn-writer is Charles Wesley and my favourite of his hymns is called 'Jesus the Name high over all'. At the end of that hymn, there is the most fantastic verse, which says:

Happy if with my latest breath,
I might but gasp His name,
Preach Him to all and cry in death,
'Behold, behold the Lamb.'

The amazing thing about Charles Wesley is that when he lay on his death-bed – having led worship thousands of times in a revival, having written hundreds of hymns – as he was about to die, he gasped 'Behold the Lamb!' What a picture for us of passion.

Now sometimes this can be a challenge, perhaps particularly for men. Matt Redman was once interviewed in *Christianity* magazine[3] about worship, and he was asked by the interviewer, 'Would you change anything in the way that you have written your songs?' Matt thought for a moment and said that he sometimes felt that he should talk more about standing in awe of God, since that is an easier concept for many men to grasp. He would still write about loving God, but would include more about being in awe of Him.

Passionate

What does it mean to be passionate in our worship? In January 1956, five missionaries entered the Ecuadorian jungle to bring the gospel to the Auca Indians. Their names were Nate Saint, Ed McCully, Jim Elliott, Roger Yoderian and Peter Fleming. Just after their arrival, the Aucas murdered them on the Curaray River. However, years later, contact with the Aucas was re-established, and many hundreds of them came to Christ – including the killers, which is how first-hand details of the missionaries' deaths came to light.

One of the five martyrs, Jim Elliot, had a saying that is still widely quoted: 'He is no fool who gives what he cannot keep, to gain what he cannot lose.' Just before their deaths these men stood together and sang the glorious hymn, 'We rest on Thee':

We rest on Thee, our Shield and our Defender!
We go not forth alone against the foe;
Strong in Thy strength, safe in Thy keeping tender,
We rest on Thee, and in Thy Name we go.
Strong in Thy strength, safe in Thy keeping tender,
We rest on Thee, and in Thy Name we go.

Yes, in Thy Name, O Captain of salvation!
In Thy dear Name, all other names above;
Jesus our Righteousness, our sure Foundation,
Our Prince of glory and our King of love.
Jesus our Righteousness, our sure Foundation,
Our Prince of glory and our King of love.

We go in faith, our own great weakness feeling,
And needing more each day Thy grace to know:
Yet from our hearts a song of triumph pealing,

We rest on Thee, and in Thy Name we go.
Yet from our hearts a song of triumph pealing,
We rest on Thee, and in Thy Name we go.

We rest on Thee, our Shield and our Defender!
Thine is the battle, Thine shall be the praise;
When passing through the gates of pearly splendour,
Victors, we rest with Thee, through endless days.
When passing through the gates of pearly splendour,
Victors, we rest with Thee, through endless days.

While still in their twenties, they were killed by the people with whom they wanted to share the good news about Jesus. Their wives and their children then carried on their work, and today many of that tribe are Christian.

There's a song for men of courage – there's a song for women as well. If you want God to stir your passion for Him in worship, think about the words that you're singing, reflect on what it actually means to devote your life to Him, and what the cost might be as well. Allow your heart to rise in praise of God as the words of the songs you sing sink in, and allow the context they were written in, or are still sung in today, to touch your heart.

Chapter 2

Deep Passion (2)

How can we stir our passion for God's word? A number of years ago, Frog and I were involved in a Bible-smuggling trip to China. We had just graduated from Oxford and he was working as a stockbroker in London. While we were working and living in London during that year, we said to the Lord, 'What do you want us to do with our holiday?' We had four weeks of holiday, and we felt the Lord say to us, 'I want you to go to China and smuggle Bibles to the suffering church there.'

It is reported that in China, every ten seconds someone becomes a Christian. There are churches of over a thousand where even the church leader does not own a personal copy of the Bible – this is the real situation. Some people point to the existence of a legal printing press in China, which prints between 1 million and 3 million Bibles each year, as evidence that Bible smuggling is not needed. However, estimates of the numbers of Christians in China range from the Communist government's figure of 15 million to the human rights agencies' figures of between 60 and 80 million. It would take many years to give every current Christian a Bible, without projecting any church growth.

Anyway, we felt the Lord was saying to us, 'Go for two weeks to China.' So Frog went into work the next day, saying, 'Please can I have these two weeks off? I'm going to China on a Bible-smuggling holiday.' And they said, 'How strange! I'm going to the Maldives.'

One of the things that *stunned* us on that trip was to briefly meet the people we were smuggling Bibles for. As members of a small team, we went on a train journey for just under twenty-four hours, we got off the train at about 4 o'clock in the morning, we walked through a town which was really off the beaten tourist track in the middle of China, and we went into a back alley for a pre-arranged meeting. We had bags filled with Bibles. Every single one of those Bibles was going to a leader of a church of over 500 people, or in some cases over 1,000.

Three Chinese men came out of the shadows. We handed over the bags, and they opened them. We will never, ever forget this moment. When they saw bags filled with Bibles in their language, they began to cry – we all cried. Such was their passion for God and His word. What a challenge to us in the Western church!

The word

Do you want to be passionate for God? Do you want to overcome Evangelical or Charismatic *ennui*? Do you want to break through that? You need to have a passion for God and a passion for reading and understanding His word. We recently heard the evangelist J. John speaking, and he said, 'If you read the Bible for fifteen minutes every day, in one year you will read the whole Bible.' Our passion for God develops as we read His word, digging deeper, hearing His wisdom in our every-day lives, saturating our minds, homes and families with the word. God's word is a beautiful thing, inspiring passion for God.

Sometimes God teaches us amazing theological truths in our Bible reading; sometimes he gives us a word for others; sometimes he gives us a prophetic word for ourselves; sometimes what we read will act as a warning to us. God's word is living and active; as we read it, He speaks to us. As we read the word, we need to remember its original context to help us interpret it correctly, but we can also read it with the expectation that God will speak to us in the here and now. This is how the great Evangelical Christians in the past, the heroes of the pulpit and missions, lived. They expected God to speak through His word.

A number of years ago we were on a mission trip in Afghanistan. We were smuggling Bibles into that country and we were trying to meet the Taliban. A rendezvous at their military headquarters had been arranged. We had to secure journalist visas to enter the country, which was gripped by a vicious civil war.

On the morning of our meeting with them, the team – Frog, myself and our friend Miles Toulmin – were completely laid out with a mysterious illness. Such was the demonic physical oppression, that we literally couldn't get out of our beds. Our backs were in spasm and we were crying out to God, asking Him what on earth was going on.

I (Amy) opened the Bible for my daily reading, and Psalm 105 was the passage I was due to read. Verses 12–13 say: 'When they were but few in number, few indeed, and strangers in it [the land], they wandered from nation to nation, from one kingdom to another.' This was what we'd done – we'd gone on a hair-raising trip from Turkmenistan through a closed border. Verse 14: 'He allowed no-one to oppress them; for their sake he rebuked kings: "Do not touch my anointed ones; do my prophets no harm."' Then, moving on, verse 30: 'Their land teemed with frogs, which went up' – wait for it! – 'which went up into the bedrooms of their rulers.'

When I saw this, I just couldn't believe it. It was there in my Bible reading! I went in and started preaching at Frog and Miles, and amazingly, they did get up. When we arrived at the military headquarters of the Taliban, we were met by the Education Minister. He took us in and we were taken through various rooms, and we sat down in their bedroom. Their sleeping mats were around the side – this was the safest bit of the building (there was still a civil war going on).

We're not offering this story as a hermeneutical tool, by the way – 'This is how to interpret the Old Testament'! What we are saying is that if we read God's word, He teaches us doctrine, correct theology, character transformation and history. But He will also stir our passion for Him and He will speak to us prophetically through His Scriptures. Try it! Read the Bible for fifteen minutes a day if you want to escape from Evangelical or Charismatic *ennui*.

As well as reading the Bible, we all need to ensure that we sit under preaching that inspires and teaches us. We have to take responsibility here for our own souls. We can find good preaching by going along and being a member of a church where there is a fantastic preaching ministry. If that is not possible, access excellent preaching on the internet and listen to it in the car, in the kitchen, whilst working out or on an errand. Make sure that you get yourself under preaching.

Today, there are a lot of people who've given up on preaching. We have seen a lot of books, articles and even seminars in the last few years saying, 'Oh, nobody can listen to preaching any more. Today's people have a twelve-minute attention span.' That's complete and utter rubbish, and needs to be rejected.

Now, it may be that they haven't heard any good preaching – fair enough! Some of the people in our church probably feel the same! But this is not a reason to give up on preaching. We need to pray for people training today at theological colleges – we should pray that formulaic and restrictive preaching training will not batter the life out of an emerging generation of preachers.

Preaching is about conviction and authority from the word being transmitted into our lives. We all need to place ourselves under that preached word. That is going to stir our fires of zeal and passion and enthusiasm.

History

We are constantly inspired to go deeper with God in this area of passion by those who have gone before us. So often we think that the things we're going through, nobody has ever been through before. If we will take the time to read Christian biographies, we will find a model for living a life of adventure, passion and zeal. Put passion into your soul through the lives of those who have gone before you.

The lives that we choose to live will, in turn, be studied by future generations. Do you want a life of significance like that? Would you like people to write on your tombstone: 'Courage, Valour, Faith'? Or do you want 'They did all right and then they died'? I know which I'd prefer.

So read about Jim Elliot in the book *Through Gates of Splendour* by Elisabeth Elliot. Read the whole history of Hudson Taylor and his amazing adventures in China. Read about George Muller and the orphanages he began in Bristol. Read about Richard Wurmbrand in Romania, enduring torture and holding onto Christ in his prison cell.

For me (Amy), reading the story of Lilias Trotter was a turning point in my life. This talented, beautiful woman wholeheartedly followed Christ and chose not to follow an obvious career path. In 1876, when Lilias was 23, she travelled with her mother to Venice, where she met the artist John Ruskin. He wrote in a letter about her:

> When I was at Venice in 1876 – it is about the only thing that makes me now content in having gone there – two English ladies, mother and daughter, were staying at the same hotel, the 'Europa'. One day the mother sent me a pretty little note asking if I would look at the young lady's drawings.
>
> On my somewhat sulky permission, a few were sent, in which I saw there was extremely right-minded and careful work, almost totally without knowledge. I sent back a request that the young lady might be allowed to come out sketching with me. She seemed to learn everything the instant she was shown it, and ever so much more than she was taught.

John Ruskin didn't believe that ladies could paint before he met Lilias. He changed his mind after he met her, and he believed that if she would devote herself to art, 'she would be the greatest living painter and do things that would be immortal.' He was unhappy that she was spending so much time on the streets of London, helping with the YWCA, when he thought she ought to be painting.

Lilias, however, decided to give up her career in art in order to serve God as a missionary in Algeria. She always remained a good friend of Ruskin, though, and they wrote many letters when she was in Algeria. She had amazing adventures amongst the Arabs as a single woman in pioneering missions work, seeing Muslims come to Christ. She was a radical, inspiring, passionate Christian.

About this decision Lilias wrote many years later:

> Never has it been so easy to live in half a dozen good harmless worlds at once – art, music, social science, games, motoring, the following of some profession, and so on. And between them we run the risk of drifting about, the 'good' hiding the 'best'.
>
> It is easy to find out whether our lives are focused, and if so, where the focus lies. Where do our thoughts settle when consciousness comes back in the morning? Where do they swing back when the pressure is off during the day? Dare to have it out with God . . . and ask Him to show you whether or not all is focused on Christ and His glory.

Action

The lack of passion can be a physical thing, as well as a mental and psychological malaise. As people sometimes say, 'I used to be apathetic, but now I just don't care.' If you're feeling apathetic, do something about it! The best way to come against apathy is action.

- One thing we can do to fire our zeal is to give exuberantly and passionately. We tithe our income at the very least, but we can give over and above that. If you want to live life on the edge, give away something that you have put aside – for example, some money to fix the roof of your house. That's what a member of our church did four years ago. Our church building was desperately run down, but people dug deep and amazed us with their passionate giving, even out of real poverty. Jesus taught that where your treasure is, there is your heart. If you've placed your treasure into the Kingdom, your heart will be there too. If you are giving exuberantly, you will feel passionate about Christ, His Kingdom and the church.

- A further action we can take is to battle with discouragement. It's interesting that the Psalmist says, 'Why so downcast, O my soul?' We are involved in a spiritual battle. In fact, the word 'downcast' refers to a sheep – the animal has fallen on its back and can't get up again. Sometimes we will feel like that, but the Psalmist encourages us to ask ourselves, 'Why so downcast, O my soul?' And then he goes on: 'Put your hope in God.' We can do battle, we can take action in our own souls.
- We can choose not to be cynical, not to mentally put our feet up, thinking, 'Yeah, yeah, impress me,' Sunday by Sunday. We can serve, we can dance.

These positive actions – giving exuberantly, battling discouragement, avoiding cynicism and even dancing before God – can stoke our passion for God.

When I (Frog) was in Uganda, I was told that when you have a small child there, it is important that you dance or dandle that child upon your knee. They said, 'It is the same when you are born again – you must learn to dance.' When you are a spiritual baby, you must learn how to dance in the Kingdom. How do we get there? The courageous Romanian church leader Richard Wurmbrand comments:

> Communists believe that happiness comes from material satisfaction, but alone in my cell, cold hungry and in rags, I

danced for joy every night. Words alone have never been able to say what man feels in the nearness of divinity. Sometimes I was so filled with joy that I felt I would burst if I didn't give it expression. I remember the words of Jesus, 'Blessed are you when men come to hate you, when they exclude you from their company and reproach you and cast out your name as evil on account of the Son of Man. Rejoice in that day and leap for joy,' and I told myself, 'I have only carried out half this command, I have rejoiced but that is not enough.' Jesus says clearly here that we must also leap and when next the guard peered through the spy-hole, he saw me springing about in my cell. His orders must have been to distract anyone who showed signs of weakness, for he padded off and returned with some food from the staff room – a hunk of bread, some cheese and some sugar, and as I took them I remembered how the verse in Luke's Gospel went on, 'Rejoice in that day and leap for joy, for behold your reward is great.' It was a very large piece of bread. I rarely allowed a night to pass then without dancing from then on, although I was never paid for it again. I made up songs and sang them softly to myself and danced to my own music. The guards became used to it, I didn't break the silence imposed on me, and they had seen many strange things in these subterranean cells. Friends to whom I spoke later of dancing in prison said, 'What for? What use was your dancing?' It wasn't something useful, it was a manifestation of joy like the dance of David, a holy sacrifice offered before the altar of the Lord. I didn't mind if my captors thought that I was mad.

Mission

If we want to be deeply passionate in mission, we should pray that God will give us a deep passion for those who don't know Christ. If we do this, we may well find that the Holy Spirit gives us groans and tears for the lost. This is something that comes from God. We may find it in our preaching, we may find it in our sharing of the word.

People used to say of George Whitefield, the famous revivalist and evangelist, 'It is hard to ignore somebody who, as they are speaking, is weeping for your soul.' Whitefield never used to preach the gospel without sobbing the appeal for people to come to Christ. He felt the deep passion of God.

I (Amy) have recently found myself welling up with tears as I preach the gospel. This can feel quite inappropriate in some contexts, like a parent and toddler service, but it is God's passion for people stirring the heart, however 'un-English' this may seem.

If we want to know passion in mission, we should pray for the lost, that they would come to know the Lord Jesus. As you do this, you may also get some wonderful by-products – for example, Frog and I met at a prayer meeting for China and Central Asia. As you pray, you begin to find the people who share your passion.

Salvation will also stoke our passion for evangelism and for mission. When you have been longing for people to come to Jesus, there is nothing more exciting than seeing them ask him into their lives. A close friend of ours prayed for years for her alcoholic, violent father to become a Christian. She cried out to God for him. Her mother and siblings had all accepted Christ, and she was now living in a faraway country, unable to see her father very often. He was diagnosed with cancer and she redoubled her prayers. All of her friends in our church began to pray for him, including our women's ministry. Close to death, he became a Christian and went on to live for another year. He was baptised at home in his old age, just weeks before he died. We all cried as she shared this story, and many women in the meeting felt a fresh passion to pray for and witness to their unbelieving family members. Salvation stirs our passion for mission, as we freshly experience the joy of people moving from darkness into light.

Early in our first year in Peckham, I (Amy) remember the culture shock of the Sunday services – it was so very different from where we'd been before. We had been praying for months that God would move in this new church we were joining to lead, praying that the lost would be saved, that many people would find Christ. We had high hopes but no idea what would happen.

One Sunday we were at the evening service with very few people there, and Frog was welcoming people as they arrived, shaking hands and chatting to them. Two young men came in, aged about 16. He shook their hands and said, 'Hello, I'm the vicar. Lovely to see you – welcome to the church.'

They explained that this was their first visit, and they mentioned where they lived – a nearby estate nicknamed 'Beirut'. They said, 'We are here because we want to be baptised.'

Frog was thrilled but wanted to make sure we were not 'sheep-stealing'. We imagined that someone had been evangelising these two guys and praying them into the Kingdom, so it would have been wrong to 'steal' them at the last minute, just as they wanted to be baptised. So Frog asked, 'How did you get to this stage, where you know Jesus and want to be baptised?'

And they said, 'Well, we've just been talking about it together and we've been thinking about it a bit, and we've prayed to Jesus, and we thought maybe we should go to church, and we just saw this church, and here we are.'

We had brought someone from Oxford to work with us and to start our youth ministry – at that time the church had just one teenager attending. So Frog called Olly to the back and he met these two guys and began to disciple them. As a result of them coming to the Lord, they brought fifteen family members and friends to our next Alpha course. They all became Christians and formed our first home group on that estate.

I can't tell you how much we rejoiced after that evening service. It didn't look good as the service was starting, in this rather dark, gloomy building in Peckham. It was raining outside and there weren't many people at the service – it was a bit depressing. But when you see people coming from darkness to light, when you see people you've longed for and prayed for coming into the Kingdom, it stokes your passion for mission.

Leadership

If you want your passion for Christ and His Kingdom to grow, you need to pray for your church leader to have that same passion. Most Christian leaders earn a shockingly low wage, which means that financial constraints are always present. Buy your leader new Christian books, buy them CDs, perhaps pay for them to go on a retreat or a conference or a holiday. The upside for you is that they will become much better at leading and they will be more passionate for God – and so will you. A passionate, encouraged leader will help you grow in passion and in encouragement. It is the experience of many church leaders that they love their church, they love the community they've been called to, but often they're really tired and a little bit discouraged, because people tend to talk to them only about the things they have found annoying or have disagreed with. Instead try to encourage your church leader.

Chapter 3

Deep Mind (1)

Many Christians today believe that if we really looked into our faith seriously, if we truly allowed our doubts or our questions to surface, then maybe we wouldn't believe any more. Suppression of these thoughts seems like the easiest option, and so they go underground. Alister McGrath comments:

> God often seems very close in the first days of faith. Yet nagging doubts sometimes remain. Can I really trust in the gospel? Surely it's just too good to be true? Does God really love me? Can I be of any use to God? Deep down, many Christians worry about questions like these, often feeling ashamed for doing so. And so they suppress them. They hope they will go away. Sometimes they do – but often they don't.[1]

As we begin this chapter we remember that Jesus said, 'Love the Lord your God with all your heart, *mind* and strength.' So, what does it mean to love God with your mind?

Worship

We think it is fair to say there is a small spat going on within churches across the country today, and on both sides of the Atlantic, and even further afield, about worship. For example, in Don Carson's anthology, *Worship by the Book*, Tim Keller writes:

> One of the basic features of church life in the United States today is the proliferation of corporate worship and music forms. This, in turn, has caused many severe conflicts within both individual congregations and whole denominations.[2]

One author has identified no fewer than eleven styles of worship in Protestantism! These include, for those who may be interested, Anabaptist, Reformed, Anglican, Lutheran, Quaker, Puritan, Methodist, Frontier and Pentecostal.[3] However, we reckon this is a huge underestimation, as we can think of at least five styles within British Evangelical Anglican worship alone! For some, the struggle or confusion is framed in terms of the tension between more formal, inherited, structured forms of worship, and the more spontaneous, free-flowing worship of the Charismatic churches – in other words, the traditional versus the renewed. For others, there is a tension between the sacramentalism and ceremony of High Church and Catholic spirituality, and the accessibility and word-based worship of Protestant churches. There is also a reaction from some quarters against what is perceived as the unhealthy emphasis on 'worship' within Charismatic churches, and they argue instead for the theological imperative to embrace worship as a life and lifestyle, not just an act of singing in church. As pastors in the lives of local congregations, we have spoken to the spiritually concerned and the basic complainers who find public worship and specifically singing a struggle. Some have been self-conscious and have claimed they sound like a broken violin when they open their mouths; others have concerns over volume or content. We remember one incident when a parishioner wrote a letter of complaint over the grammar in one of the favourite songs sung in the youth group. (Yes – it was Oxford!)

The phrase 'Deep Church', as we said in the Introduction, is in part about emphasising that we need not exclude what is precious or biblical because of the latest fad, nor do we need to reject what is already established as useful, good and scriptural. Tim Keller again:

> I believe the solution to the problem of the 'worship wars' is neither to reject nor to enshrine historic tradition but to forge new forms of corporate worship that take seriously both our histories and contemporary realities.[4]

In authentic worship we are called to engage our minds *and* be sensitive to the leading and experience of the Holy Spirit; to healthily mark the interplay between our life journey *and* our faith journey through the sacraments of Holy Communion and Baptism, which we share together in the life of a local congregation. And though it is right to declare that worship is a lifestyle and not just about singing, it is hard to escape the weight of Scripture itself on the subject. Worship *is* a lot about singing.

Take the Psalms as examples – an entire book of worship songs, filled with exhortations to worship, using music and voice:

> Sing to God, O kingdoms of the earth, sing praise to the Lord.
> Psalm 68:32

Sing to the LORD a new song; sing to the LORD, all the earth.

Psalm 96:1

I will sing of your love and justice; to you, O LORD, I will sing praise.

Psalm 101:1

I will sing to the LORD all my life; I will sing praise to my God as long as I live.

Psalm 104:33

Sing to God, sing praise to his name, extol him who rides on the clouds – his name is the LORD – and rejoice before him.

Psalm 68:4

May they sing of the ways of the LORD, for the glory of the LORD is great.

Psalm 138:5

Rejoice in the LORD and be glad, you righteous; sing, all you who are upright in heart!

Psalm 32:11

Sing to the LORD with thanksgiving; make music to our God on the harp.

Psalm 147:7

The call to worship by singing also comes to us from God through the prophets:

Sing to the LORD! Give praise to the LORD! He rescues the life of the needy from the hands of the wicked.

Jeremiah 20:13

Sing to the LORD, for he has done glorious things; let this be known to all the world.

Isaiah 12:5

The call to worship by singing to God comes to us today through historical books and examples:

Miriam sang to them: 'Sing to the LORD, for he is highly exalted. The horse and its rider he has hurled into the sea.'

Exodus 15:21

After consulting the people, Jehoshaphat appointed men to sing to the LORD and to praise him for the splendour of his holiness as they went out at the head of the army, saying: 'Give thanks to the LORD, for his love endures forever.'

2 Chronicles 20:21

Hear this, you kings! Listen, you rulers! I will sing to the LORD, I will sing; I will make music to the LORD, the God of Israel.

Judges 5:3

The New Testament letters echo the Old Testament's call to worship by singing:

Speak to one another with psalms, hymns and spiritual songs. Sing and make music in your heart to the Lord.

Ephesians 5:19

The absence of worship and singing is a sign of spiritual dereliction and despair:

By the rivers of Babylon we sat and wept when we
    remembered Zion.
There on the poplars we hung our harps,

for there our captors asked us for songs,
our tormentors demanded songs of joy;
they said, 'Sing us one of the songs of Zion!'
How can we sing the songs of the LORD
while in a foreign land?

Psalm 137:41–44

Though there can be moments when the rational, think-ing part of us moves to the back seat, this is neither nec-essary, nor perhaps desirable in either private or public worship. In fact, the thoughtfulness of worship through singing is made all the more real through the examples of singing in the extremities of life. The apostles sing worship even when in prison, and Jesus himself sings Psalms. He even uses the words of Psalm 22:1 while suf-fering on the cross:

About the ninth hour Jesus cried out in a loud voice, *'Eloi, Eloi, lama sabachthani?'* – which means, 'My God, my God, why have you forsaken me?'

Matthew 27:46

The prophet Habakkuk is a man struggling with a sense of injustice and disillusionment. His book is filled with carefully constructed moral and political complaints against God. As he realises that he may have more times of hardship and struggle ahead, he finishes the proph-ecy with a prayer, but one designed to be sung publicly, not only by him, but also by congregations for years to come:

Though the fig tree does not bud
and there are no grapes on the vines,
though the olive crop fails
and the fields produce no food,

though there are no sheep in the pen
and no cattle in the stalls,
yet I will rejoice in the LORD,
I will be joyful in God my Saviour.
The Sovereign LORD is my strength;
he makes my feet like the feet of a deer,
he enables me to go on the heights.

Habakkuk 3:17–19

When we're looking at the concept of worship from the perspective of the mind, we want to ask you this question: when you are worshipping, what are you thinking about? As I (Amy) was first preparing this material, I found myself about two days afterwards on the front row of our church, All Saints. We have a big dome at the front and there's a small patch in the dome which lets water in, and the plaster has become cracked. We've tried to repair it once and now the crack is beginning to come through again. So while we were worshipping I was looking at that and thinking, 'I wonder what it would take to get that fixed', and then I found myself thinking, 'Oh my goodness, I've got twenty-five people coming for lunch and I forgot to turn the oven on! What are we going to eat?!' I hasten to add that this is an exception rather than the rule, since I really love worshipping in church and totally focusing on the words. But it stands out in my mind as something we all slip into sometimes.

What are you thinking about when you worship? If you have been a Christian for longer than five years, you may be singing a song for literally the thousandth time, and so there is an inevitable familiarity about the words. As someone who grew up in a Christian home and who has been to church every Sunday, often twice, for over thirty years, I believe it is crucially important that we equip ourselves to worship in song with our minds as well as our hearts. In fact, when our minds are enlivened through worship, passion rises up in our hearts once again.

One of the most significant things we can begin to do as thinking Christians is to contemplate the layers of meaning and the theology of the songs that we're singing. Think about the songs that you sing as you sing them. Allow the Lord to touch your heart and your spirit, but also your mind. Really reflect on the concepts you are singing about.

We were recently singing the song 'Jesus you are worthy' and were especially impacted by the bridge section:

Worthy is the Lamb that once was slain
To receive all glory, power and praise,
For with Your blood You purchased us for God:
Jesus, You are worthy,
That is what You are.
Perfect sacrifice,
Crushed by God for us,
Bearing in Your hurt all that I deserve.
Misjudged for my misdeeds,
You suffered silently,
The only guiltless man in all of history.

Brenton Brown & Don Williams,
© *2005 Thankyou Music*

This is profound theology exploring the nature of the atonement. Declaring that He is the only guiltless man in all history grounds our worship in the transaction of guilty lives swapped for a guiltless one. Within this song is a tight biblical theology of justification ('misjudged for my misdeeds'), penal substitution ('crushed by God for us'), sacrifice ('Lamb that once was slain') and redemption ('purchased us for God') – theological models of the atonement brought to life in song.

Sometimes it's important to think about the layers of meaning in the songs or even the context that songs are sung in. The worship leader and song-writer Matt Redman was asked in an interview which was his favourite song in his album *Beautiful News*, and he replied:

> I'd have to say 'You never let go'. My wife Beth and I wrote it during the week of the London bombings in July 2005. In the same week she had suffered a miscarriage – it was just one of those times where your whole world seems to be breaking and shaking apart and you just can't make sense of it. In times like those we need some unshakeable truth to stand on – and that was the whole heart-cry behind this song – we were clinging on to the truth of a God who never lets us go. The really wonderful thing is that during the recording of the album Beth was pregnant again. After one of the scans we wrote the song 'Fearfully and wonderfully made' together, which also appears on the album. Last September Beth gave birth to our fantastic little son Rocco Benjamin, and we're so massively grateful to God for His kindness.[5]

In our church we have an amazing group of ladies, some of whom have been members of All Saints for over thirty years, but ten years ago they really *were* the church. As they prayed weekly, and met together and sang, it became clear that without a move of God, there seemed to be little hope for growth. The Diocese made a deal with the council to sell and redevelop the land: they were going to bulldoze our Victorian church. Our predecessor, Bob Hurley, came into that context, and these ladies, who had been faithfully praying whilst seeing nothing but decline, experienced a wonderful renewal as people began to join the church. One of their favourite hymns is 'Leaning on the everlasting arms'. Now two of these women regularly walk around Peckham, and if they see a gang fight happening on their estate or somewhere they're walking, they don't run away and hide. These ladies are well into their latter years, but they go in there and they break up these groups of young people who are fighting and they tell them, 'Go home! What would your mother think about you doing this? Jesus doesn't want you to be doing this!' The last verse of their favourite hymn is:

What have I to dread, what have I to fear?
Leaning on the everlasting arms,
I have precious peace
With my Lord so near,
Leaning on the everlasting arms.

Now every time I sing that hymn, I think about those women fearlessly walking the streets of Peckham, and I feel inspired by their example to live boldly and courageously for the Lord. The context of a song can help us to see the layers of meaning in it and to more deeply engage our minds as we sing.

When we were in Oxford we worked with a wonderful couple called John and Sue Chorlton who headed up the pastoral ministry in that church. John knew the detail of the difficult situations in the congregation members' lives. He knew their struggles, he knew their tragedies, he knew their broken-heartedness, and his favourite song was:

I will lift the name of Jesus up high, lift his name up high,
I will lift the name of Jesus up high, lift his name up high.

A thousand angels singing round the throne,
Giving the glory to the King,
And now we join with them, our voices raised,
Proclaiming Jesus – His mighty name we sing.

He sang that over all of those situations. We need to think about what we sing, so as to engage our minds in worship.

We also suggest that to worship God with our minds involves thinking about real-life issues in a Christian way. Having the mind of God concerning the situations in which we live is to worship with our minds. What does it mean to think Christianly about the difficult issues that we face? If our minds are renewed, we will think about situations differently from the world around us. In the world, if someone hurts you, the logical response is to take revenge or to get away from the aggressor and resent them in your heart. For the Christian, the way we are to think about this kind of situation is completely different.

A good friend of ours was worshipping in a church in Indonesia when some grenades were thrown into the building by a group of Islamists. The congregation members ran out of the church because it was on fire, and there were militants waiting for them and shooting the people as they ran out of the church.

Someone got hold of our friend as she was running away, and he put the barrel of a gun to her face and said, 'Renounce Jesus or die!'

She said, 'I could never renounce Jesus. I love Him – He's saved me!' So the man pulled the trigger. Half of her face was blown off but she survived.

Afterwards she was asked by another friend of ours, Michael Ramsden, 'How do you feel about the people who did this to you?'

She replied, 'Well, I must love them and forgive them because that's what Jesus calls us to do. That's what He did.'

'Are you able to work?' asked Michael.

'No, I can't really work, but what I do now is to make up packages of food and aid, and I take them to the community where these militants came from. I go and find their mothers and their aunts and their uncles and their sisters, and I say to them, "Have this gift in the name of Jesus."'

What an amazing woman! Here is an example of someone who has a Christian mind – her pattern of thinking and her actions which follow are renewed by Christ. She is someone who worships Christ with her mind and her attitudes.

The word

One of the things that I (Frog) was aware of when I went up to university was the mismatch between my thinking about other things and my thinking about Christianity. My Christian thoughts were fragmented and narrowly focused on religious items. We can easily find ourselves excelling in our studies or workplace, specialising in what we know professionally, but never getting near that level when it comes to the Bible. It may be that in the workplace we know everything there is to know about how to make an Excel spreadsheet, but when it comes to 'How does the Bible fit together?' we think, 'Oh, I don't know. I'm not really a theologian. I don't really see myself as an expert in that way.' And we find ourselves in the situation I found myself in a few years ago, where our non-Christian thinking is better than our Christian thinking. We have developed skills of the mind, which we are applying in the workplace, but we have allowed our thoughts about God, his word and the universe to atrophy, wither and die. Imagine somebody who's a tennis player, and they've always been playing with their right hand, and their left arm is frail, because they haven't used it. Sometimes our minds can become like that. We have been using our brains, but when it comes to thinking thoughts which chase after God, that's become a weak hand, and we let other people do the work for us.

So how we can be passionate and deep when it comes to the word? If we want to pursue this idea of a deep mind and deep thinking, Colossians has some powerful insights for us. In Colossians 1:21 we read, 'Once you were alienated from God and were enemies' – where? – 'in your *minds*.' Look at the whole verse again:

> Once you were alienated from God and were enemies in your minds because of your evil behaviour, but now he has reconciled you by Christ's physical body through death, to make you holy in his sight.

And in Colossians 2:2–4 we read:

> My purpose is that they may be encouraged in heart and united in love, so that they may have the full riches of complete understanding, in order that they may know the mystery of God, namely Christ, in whom are hidden all the treasures of wisdom and knowledge. I tell you this so that no one may deceive you by fine-sounding arguments.

It is the genuine, personal, real and fulfilling relationship with the Person of Christ which equips us so that we are not deceived by fine-sounding arguments, which try to drag us away from God. There may well be many fine-sounding arguments out there, but we aren't to be deceived by them. We can be protected from this deception by being completely rooted in and filled by Christ. Paul goes on in this theme (Col. 2:8):

> See to it that no-one takes you captive through hollow and deceptive philosophies which depend on human traditions and the basic principles of this world, rather than on Christ, for in Christ all the fullness of the deity lives in bodily form.
>
> Colossians 2:8

Who is that addressed to? Us. This is addressed not to sceptical unbelievers but to true Christians. We Christians need to watch out that we are not taken captive by 'hollow and deceptive philosophy' – that is, wrong ideas about God and His world. We may often think of spiritual warfare as demons in the rafters, but frequently the enemy is using an argument or an idea. You can't cast out an argument. You can try, but it won't be very effective. Paul is using words that have a spiritual authority and power here, as he is talking about our minds: *captivity, slavery* and *freedom* all emphasise that there is battle over the mind.

We have so often 'spiritualised' the spiritual battle, and in so doing we don't realise how much of it is going on in our own mind. It may be something as simple and profound as the concept of being loved by God the Father. We know that God loves people and we see it in Scripture, and yet our minds are still taken captive by the idea that we are unloved, and so we're living as if we are fatherless. We are living as if we have got to prove something to our heavenly Father.

But the word says that we are loved, that we have nothing to prove, that we're accepted by grace, that we are adopted into his family and that he says: 'I love you.

I loved you before you even did anything for my Kingdom; when you were still a sinner, I loved you.' That's what the word says. And so when our heart is saying, 'I'm unloved', our deeply renewed mind can correct our heart and put it on track again. But this is only possible if we are bringing our minds into contact with God's word.

Preaching

But how can we respond to this pro-actively other than by reading the word for ourselves? As we have already suggested, we need to recapture the crucial life-giving role of preaching in our churches. We need preaching which is passionate and engaging of the heart, but we also need our minds to be trained and stretched through the preached word. Sometimes we don't like taking physical exercise because of the effort, discomfort and even pain involved. But we do it because our bodies need that order and discipline to stay strong and keep functioning with the pace of our lives. There is a huge focus on this kind of fitness in our society – even the non-Christian world agrees on the importance of this, but as Christians we believe that our minds also need training. Even though we are born again in a moment and our whole being is changed as soon as we ask Jesus into our life, the renewal of our mind is a process.

This mind renewal can most significantly happen as we listen to and are challenged by thoughtful, biblical, anointed preaching. Unfortunately, some in our churches think that the days of preaching are gone, and that it is no longer useful in a society such as ours. John Stott comments:

The contemporary world is decidedly unfriendly towards preaching. Words have been largely eclipsed by images, and the book by the screen. So preaching is regarded as an outmoded form of communication, what someone has called 'an echo from an outmoded past'. Who want to listen to sermons nowadays? People are drugged by television, hostile to authority and suspicious of words.[6]

It has never been more urgent than it is now to redress the balance of disillusionment with preaching, replacing this *ennui* with a resurgent hunger for fire and light to come to us through the preached word. Charles Spurgeon said: 'there must be light as well as fire. Some preachers are all light and no fire, while others are all fire and no light. What we want is both fire and light.'[7] Preaching, said Martyn Lloyd-Jones, is 'theology coming through a man who is on fire'.[8] Dietrich Bonhoeffer, a German pastor and theologian who was killed by Hitler's regime, speaks of the living encounter with Jesus through preaching as 'not a medium of expression for something else, something that lies behind it, but rather it is Christ himself, walking through his congregation as the Word.'[9]

Is this our experience? Perhaps we have never heard a sermon that grabs us and truly impacts us, so that we think as we listen, 'This is the word of God eternal and the word of God for me today!' That is what preaching is meant to be – spoken and received as if it were the very words of God.

Why might we not value preaching? Some suggest that preaching gets in the way of the truly spiritual moments of worship, and that it affects only our rational, intellectual selves. Some see it as out of date, whereas others suggest that preaching is just for well-educated types. The theologian Ian Stackhouse

suggests many Charismatic churches are drifting away
from this important ministry:

> Thus, even where there is a healthy regard for preaching,
> for example, as might exist among Reformed Charismatics,
> there is often a nagging sense that if one were to be truly
> open to the Spirit, one would not be taking up so much
> time sermonising, let alone devoting oneself to the public
> reading of Scripture.[10]

Equally damaging is the widespread approach to training which teaches that the only way to preach genuinely biblical sermons is to follow a narrow, stylised
model of exposition. The great Evangelical preachers of
the past never conformed to any of these 'rules' for
preaching and actually worked in a far more dynamic,
intuitive and prophetic way. Charles Spurgeon describes
words of knowledge in sermons, and the Reformers of
Edward VI's reign used to get together for 'prophesy-
ings' – which Queen Elizabeth later banned!

My (Amy's) father was ministering in an inner-city
church in Birmingham for a long time. It was often
assumed that since the people there were poorly educated or on the margins of society in some way, he would
only preach for five minutes, because, surely, such people
would have a short attention span. And he would dis-
agree, saying, 'No! Why should people who didn't have
a good education be denied the word of God?' He found
that, through the power of the Holy Spirit, their attention
span grew, and they learned how to learn. They got
excited about the word, often weeping during forty-
minute-long meaty sermons. Young men would sit still,
completely thrilled by a sermon on Romans.

We preachers need to actually engage our brains, put
in serious preparation and go deeper with our words.

One of the temptations and pressures you can sometimes feel as a preacher is to always try to preach a word that demands an immediate response. Perhaps, if I know I'm going to get 400 people coming forward for prayer ministry, I will have this inner glow and satisfaction that I've preached a sound word. Whereas if I explain the Creed, which is vitally important in today's church, I might not get that kind of response.

Sometimes there can be an implicit, psychological pressure on the preacher to always preach for an emotional response, when we need the mind to be taught and challenged through the preached word. All Christians need to understand how the word fits together, we all need to go deeper in doctrine if we are to have the mind of Christ, we all need to explore the serious apologetic questions which outsiders ask, we all need to understand eschatology and judgement, we all need to be aware of atonement theology. But of course, it is much more fun to get a hundred people coming up and saying, 'Oh, bless me, Lord!' with tears pouring down their faces.

We are not denying the need for passion in preaching – we wholeheartedly believe in that. We love to call people to respond to God's word with genuine emotion, but this does not have to be at the expense of serious, biblical, thoughtful preaching. We can have both. Evangelicals have always had both in the past, and there is no reason to let go of this vision of a deep mind at this point in history.

We should also be wary of those who want to see an end to the preached word. Just because some preaching is of a low standard does not mean that we should dispense with all preaching. On the contrary, our generation desperately needs the preached word, Sunday by Sunday, if we are to have deep minds.

We who are involved in preaching and teaching, whether that be in small groups or in our churches, need to be encouraged to continue with this vital work. John Stott used to preach on the Thirty-Nine Articles of the Anglican faith and the Creed every couple of years in his ministry at All Souls Langham Place. He thought it was important to do that. He is famous as a Bible teacher and we have been really inspired by that.

Some of us may suffer from a sense of inferiority. Perhaps we feel that we are thick, and so when anything that sounds like a long word comes up in a sermon, we disqualify ourselves and switch off from listening. Or if anything sounds even remotely intellectual, we don't want to fail to understand it, so we decide not to try at all. If we want to worship God and have a depth in our thinking, we need to ask for the Holy Spirit's help in this area. God wants to change and transform us.

As a teenager I (Frog) was renowned as being one of the most scatty people in the universe. I led a social-whirlwind existence, attending two or three events in succession to pack it all into one evening – forgetting details, directions, thank-you letters and keys. As a Christian in training for leadership, I needed to pray about that. I thought, 'Well, I can't carry on being completely scatty and always turning up for everything late and triple- and quadruple-booking myself – I need help here.' The report written on me when leaving theological college commended my administration skills, which really was a miraculous turn-around!

We have a friend, Mick, who was involved in a motor-bike accident many years ago, and as a result of this he completely lost all memory. He had never been great at reading but after the accident, he had no ability to read. He became a Christian a few years ago, and he thought, 'Well, if I'm a Christian, I want to understand the word of God.' So he prayed, and he decided to learn how to read so that he could read the Bible. He is now the verger in our church. He saw how important reading God's word was, and so took action. Well, maybe we need to do something similar.

We have met teachers in Uganda who talk about the problems of overcrowding in their education system. There are people hiding in cupboards in the schoolroom overnight so they can sneak into the classroom in the morning. They can't afford to pay for the education, but they are so desperate to learn to read that they will do anything to get to a lesson. Teachers there wonder how to deal with the twenty children outside the classroom window who are listening to the lesson from the branches of trees. We so easily take the things that are given to us for granted. We are squandering our education and allowing our brains to atrophy, and this is not glorifying to God.

A further way of developing a deep mind as a Christian is to begin to gain a broader perspective on the word – remembering that God's word is the word for the world, not just for the West. A few years ago we had a great opportunity to go to China and to minister with fellow university students. We travelled throughout China but spent a longer period of time in Xinchiang province, which is the far north-west of the country, home of a Muslim people called the Uyghurs.

We led some English conversation classes at the university in a city called Urumqi. On our last evening there, we went back to our hotel, and Amy said, 'There was this girl in my group, and I just saw a look on her face, and I thought, "She wants to ask me about Christianity", but she just couldn't get it out.' So we sat in the grotty stairwell of the hotel, and we started to pray for this girl, that God would intervene in her life.

And as we prayed, we started to weep for her – we started to feel God's desire for her to come into relationship with Him. We laid it before God and we went out for supper.

That night we were meeting up with an undercover missionary. We wanted to take him out for a meal to encourage him and pray for him and to have fellowship together. He had worked in the Islamic world for about seventeen years sharing the gospel, and he'd been thrown out of numerous countries, but he was spending a year in this particular area while we happened to be passing through.

As we sat and ate together in the restaurant, we asked him what organisation he worked with, and he wrote it down on a little piece of paper and showed it to us in silence. Then he ripped it up into tiny pieces and we almost expected him to swallow it! It was a fascinating insight into undercover missions work and the kind of life he was living for Jesus in that difficult situation.

At the end of the meal he gave us two Uyghur John's Gospels. We were reluctant to take them, as they were so difficult to get hold of locally and we were unlikely to meet any more local people, as we were about to leave. But he insisted on giving them to us, as he felt that the Lord had told him to do this.

The next day, at about ten o'clock in the morning, the phone in our hotel room rang. There were two Uyghur girls downstairs wanting to meet with Amy, and the receptionist handed the phone to one of them. In broken English, the girl said she had dreamed the previous night that Jesus had said to her, 'Speak to that woman you met today. She has something to tell you about God and getting to know God better.'

Ten other students from the previous day's conversation class had also turned up at the hotel. Among them was someone who was likely to be a government informer. We put the group of ten into one room and Amy took these two girls into another room. We had stored the two Uyghur Gospels in this room the night before, and so Amy was then able to give them to the girls!

We have this treasure, this wisdom of God, and so often we don't put our energy into going deeper into it – when there are other people, who might need a bunch of students to be flung to the far side of the world, and dreams and prayers and prophecies, in order for them to even get a Gospel into their hands. What a contrast!

Chapter 4

Deep Mind (2)

Some of the great thinkers of the past have been committed Christians – for example, the mathematician Pascal and the physicist Newton. Reading history involves reading their thoughts and reflecting on them.

History

Saint Augustine (354–430) developed what might now be called a coherent worldview. As a preacher and church leader, he wrote on psychology, politics, economics, the environment, science, philosophy, law, morality, history, pastoral care, worship and spirituality. He was thinking and writing in a Western cultural context which bears some similarity to ours today. He had a later-life conversion experience and wrote theology in a contested environment where pluralism ruled and many thinking people thought that Christianity was intellectually incoherent. Before his conversion, Augustine himself had rather looked down his nose at Christianity because the Latin text of the Bible (the Vulgate, put together by early missionaries from the Greek text) was such a poor translation. Later he became a bishop and theologian in North Africa. His key books include his autobiography, *The Confessions*; a work of political philosophy, *The City of God*; and a master-work on psychology and the doctrine of God, *On the Trinity*. To read Augustine is to develop the Christian mind.

Thomas Aquinas (1225–74) was an epoch-making theologian who wrote on prayer, ethics, philosophy and the doctrine of the church. Thomism is the school of thought named after him which dominated European culture in the Middle Ages. He developed five arguments for the existence of God, as well as principles of analogy which provide a theological framework for revelation through the creation. His key works include *Summa Contra Gentiles* and *Summa Theologiae*. He is surprisingly easy to read in English and is an inspiring Christian thinker.

Martin Luther (1483–1546), a German ex-monk, shook the world by recapturing the doctrine of justification by faith and placing the Scriptures into the hands of ordinary Germans, with a punchy translation of the New Testament. From the time he banged his 'ninety-five theses' onto the wooden doors of a church in Wittenberg, the Reformation never looked back. He articulated a non-legalistic gospel, developed a theology of the church and state, and wrote witheringly on the abuse of power. His main works include *The Ninety-Five Theses*, *The Babylonian Captivity of the Church*, and his sermons and commentaries. Luther passionately envisaged a Bible in the hands of every Christian, theology taken out of the clutches of experts and given to the whole church, and the development of the Christian mind for every believer.

John Calvin (1509–64), a French Reformer, was converted in his mid twenties and went on to become one of the key thinkers and leaders of the second wave of the European Reformation. Most of the ideas in the later

English Reformation are modelled on his thought, which is reflected in the *Book of Common Prayer*. His impact was felt most in Geneva and Strasbourg where he exercised roles in leadership, spiritual oversight and teaching. Thus his thinking on politics, society and systematic theology, though governed by Scripture, was grounded in the day-to-day experiences of church and city life. His main works are the *Institutes*, and his sermons and commentaries. Alister McGrath says 'Calvinism is still one of the most potent and significant intellectual movements in human history.'[1]

John Bunyan (1628–88), one-time soldier and then English Baptist preacher and pastor, wrote *The Pilgrim's Progress* (Part 1, 1678; Part 2, 1684) after a twelve-year prison sentence. For a century it was the best-selling book in English, second only to the Bible. An allegory of discipleship, it remains a spiritual classic and a thoroughly good read. Through it we get phrases such as 'Vanity Fair' and the 'Slough of Despond', and some would argue that it was also the beginning of the English novel. One of his other books, *The Holy War*, is a superb study on what we might today call inner healing or the spiritual battle as it applies to the individual.

Foxe's Book of Martyrs (by John Foxe, 1517–87) stands alongside *The Pilgrim's Progress* as an account of Christian martyrs, and was a profound history and theology teacher to generations of Protestants. It retells the stories of courageous Christian deaths at the hands of persecutors from the first century until the sixteenth, and is a crucial read. It was often found chained to the pulpit so that people could read it in village churches across England, and the arguments within it were said to have convinced Queen Elizabeth to move towards an end to executions for religious crimes. Develop your Christian mind by becoming conversant with these stories.

Jonathan Edwards is perhaps America's foremost Christian philosopher. One editor went as far as to say in 1898: 'By Universal confession of the princeliest leaders in the world of thought, Jonathan Edwards must be included among those whose gifts are of the supremest sort.'[2] Edwards oversaw a revival in Northampton, USA, in 1740–42, but his account of the events and conversions and his theological reflection upon what he had witnessed really marked him out as a giant in the fields of philosophy, ethics, psychology and theology. His key works are *A Narrative of Surprising Conversions, An Account of the Revival of Religion in Northampton 1740–42, The Religious Affections* and *On Knowing Christ*. If you want to be a person who experiences the power of the Spirit and the stretching of your mind at the same time, may Jonathan Edwards become your trainer.

There are several twentieth-century English-speaking authors whose writings are important, influential and accessible, whom we also recommend: namely, C.S. Lewis, Dorothy L. Sayers, G.K. Chesterton and Francis Schaeffer. (We are also huge fans of Solzhenitsyn and Tolstoy.) With the exception of Schaeffer, who was more of a cultural commentator and apologist, these writers bridged the gap between theology and the modern mind with a keen insight into literature and popular culture. With others such as J.R.R. Tolkien, they expressed the Christian view of the world convincingly to a newly non-Christian West.

C.S. Lewis wrote not only great stories for children (the Narnia Chronicles) and adults (his science-fiction trilogy), but also *Mere Christianity, God in the Dock* and *The Screwtape Letters*. Some of these books first appeared as radio programmes, as did Sayers' biblical play, *The Man Who Would be King*. Chesterton's works did battle with the newspapers and made witty and persuasive arguments in favour of a Christian faith that didn't need to adapt its content to suit the day, but perhaps only its communication (see his books *Orthodoxy*, *Heretics* and the *Everlasting Man*).

Schaeffer championed the importance of the Christian mind and encouraged thoughtful Christianity in the face of the dominant thought-systems of the contemporary world, especially as expressed through philosophy, popular music and fine art. He encouraged people to examine their assumptions and presuppositions, whether followers of Christ or not, and to have a consistent worldview, believing that this would help those inside and outside the church. He suggested that a natural outworking of the underlying planks of many views of reality found outside God would lead to despair, and that we should not be afraid to go there. Essentially, he argued, life without God may seem despairing and meaningless, and reconnecting with our Creator through Christ restores our innate purpose, identity and destiny.

A worldview is simply a unifying set of assumptions, a grid, or a set of truths that helps you to think about the world. If we are to be deep in this area of the mind, we need to begin to think Christianly about every area of life, including our very framework of thought about reality. There are four key headings when it comes to worldview, which are origin, meaning, morality and destiny. If we think Christianly and correctly about those things, that will have an impact on our whole life, both day to day, and the big picture.

Origin

The Christian believes that every human being is precious to God because He has made humans beings in His image. This is in huge contrast to the other worldviews around us, whether they be atheism (which believes that human life is just the product of matter, time and chance, a species in which all compete and the strong take precedence over the weak), or pantheism (that's the worldview behind Buddhism and Hinduism, which teaches that humankind isn't created in the image of God, but that all people are actually mere illusions of one impersonal, ultimate reality). A great debate has raged in India over the involvement of Christians in poverty relief, since pantheism does not lead to the valuing of individuals and the upholding of life. The belief that humans are created in God's image is a fundamental belief about the origin of life that has motivated Christian social action for two thousand years. Life is precious because God is the author of life.

Meaning

The existentialist writer Albert Camus, who argued that God does not exist, wrote:

> There is one truly philosophical problem and that is suicide. Judging whether life is or is not worthy of living amounts to answering the fundamental question of philosophy. I see many people die, i.e. commit suicide, because they judge that life is not worth living. I see others, paradoxically, getting killed for the ideas or illusions that give them a reason for living. And what is called a reason for living is also an excellent reason for dying.

Our Christian brothers and sisters who are suffering for their faith would agree with that. If you are an atheist, there is no meaning. There is no purpose to life. Suicide is a logical by-product of that. But relationship with God is the purpose of life – and one which is worth dying for.

Morality

How do I conduct my actions? Am I just a victim, a product of my environment? Is there a God who gives us a moral law by which to order our lives? Are we morally responsible for hurting others and our environment? Will we be held to account for that? What we believe about moral accountability has a massive impact on how we live. If you believe that God exists and that He has morally ordered the universe, that is going to massively impact how you live, and how you order the society that you live in.

Destiny

What is the ultimate end of human beings? Is it just 'today we live and tomorrow we die', or is there a life beyond the grave that means it is worth giving ourselves in the cause of others so that they might meet Jesus and be with him beyond the grave? Is it worth living for an eternal reward? There is a life beyond this life, therefore I don't just live for my own material comfort; I live for the sake of Jesus and for the sake of others, because one day we will be with Him. Many of us in the church have lost that clear orientation.

History can be a useful corrective to the faddishness of a contemporary church blown this way and that by the newest theological techniques, which promise so much but deliver so little.

Action

What needs to change in our lives so that we can go deeper with God using our minds? One of the things we can do at a practical level is to study. We can actively pursue the development and the renewal of our Christian mind and our Christian thinking. That will take time. I remember reading a children's book about a monkey who was very keen to become intelligent, and he saw that lots of information was in books, and he thought that the best thing to do was to rip up a book into lots of small pieces and to eat them. If only it were as easy as eating a few mouthfuls – unfortunately it will take more work than that. However, it does not have to necessarily involve a formal university education. We can develop our Christian mind by reading and studying. The core areas of biblical studies are the Old and New Testaments, Doctrine, Church History, Missionary Biography, Apologetics – and first and foremost, the word of God itself. There is action that we can take. There is something we can do about it. We are not helpless. We can study.

Secondly, there's action in terms of using the mind for strategy. Vision comes from the Lord but it needs to be implemented. The Lord often prophetically gives us strategies to help us fulfil the vision. But alongside this, He also calls us to use the resources He has entrusted us with. Strategic thinking is working out a plan of how we get from where we are to where we want to be. This process can and should be Spirit inspired. We are constantly thinking strategically, asking the Holy Spirit to influence our strategy. In fact, the five years that we have been in Peckham have stretched us both to absolute breaking-point in our thinking. For us as leaders, this means using our minds and all of the training that we have been given to work hard ourselves, but also to clearly lead our team to work in the harvest-field using every capacity we have.

With pioneer mission, if we want to break into a new community or a new group, or a school, we have to work out a plan to initiate an evangelistic work, and we need to plan beforehand – how can we grow that work once we're there? Strategic thinking means using all of our creative, analytical and planning skills to the max *before* as well as *during* the establishing of a work. Key questions which require practical answers include: What form will our mission take – a club, a group, an activity? Who are we hoping to reach? What are their practical and spiritual needs? Who will lead this work? What are their gifts and skills? Who will be in the team? What form will the evangelism take? How will we disciple the new followers of Jesus who will be the result of the work? How will we keep the pioneering work going? How can we make sure that once we've had a breakthrough, it doesn't all wither and suddenly go back to chaos again?

An example for us in Peckham has involved a school in our community. It's a new City Academy, and All Saints had been helping run a Christian club at lunchtime for a few years in the school. But we had a vision to grow the work in this school on our doorstep. Following several meetings with the headmaster, I (Frog) brought to him the idea of having someone working in the school, paid by the church. The headmaster suggested the job title of Academy Pastor. We were wanting to see a youth church planted into the school, Christian pastoral care given to young people and help offered in every academic subject, but especially religious and social education. The title seemed to encapsulate our vision perfectly. This role is now in its third year, the Academy church meets once a week, mentoring schemes are established, and there are two other weekly prayer meetings as well.

Thirdly, we can take action through negotiation. This entails understanding people, communicating well and moving the things of God forward. At the beginning of our time in Peckham we had a vision to bring five or six people to come and live in a house in Peckham and work full tilt as missionaries. We thought, why not ask some of our Oxford students who felt called into missions to come and live as a missionary in the urban jungle for a year or two, rather than the jungles of South America, and they said 'Yes!'

We had appointed six people to start in September; we arrived in May without a single penny to go on. We just knew that the Lord was leading us and that He would provide. I remember going to our first fund-raising meeting with a charity. This charity was actually a Christian one, and in our discussions with them they said, 'You live in a very multicultural area, with lots of different religions. Before we look at giving you money or making this approval, we want an assurance from you that you would not seek to proselytise under any circumstances.'

So I prayed, 'God, give us the answer in this. Help me to think Christianly in this area of negotiation.' I said, 'Am I to understand, therefore, that you have a policy of discrimination against Evangelical Christians such as myself?'

And they said, 'What do you mean?'

I said, 'We don't believe in discrimination. We try to share the good news about Jesus with everybody, and to practise no discrimination whatsoever in who we present that good news to, whatever colour, nationality or religious background they may come from. Are you saying therefore that you have discrimination as a policy built into the way that you give out your money, that you cannot give it to us because of our religion?'

And they said, 'No, no, no – of course not! Of course we don't discriminate.'

And after that they made the recommendation, and we've received money from them ever since. We all need to ask the Lord for His help as we negotiate – but we must also use our minds in this area.

Mission

So much of our actions pertain to mission, but on top of all of this, 1 Peter 3:15 says: 'In your hearts set apart Christ as Lord and always be prepared to give an answer for the reason for the hope that you have.' Having a good answer to the questions of sceptics is not something that we leave to the experts. All of us are to be involved in this task of apologetics, day to day. Peter's letter is written to the whole church, not just to clever people, or evangelists, or confident people. Peter's words come to every single one of us. Being obedient to this will involve us using and training our minds. We may be giving an answer about the Christian faith to people we meet who we have had no previous contact with, people who are just strangers. For some of us, it will primarily be people who are close, like our children, our parents, our neighbours, or our close friends. We may need to be proactive and ask them questions like: 'Are there any reasons why you are not a Christian?' so that we can know where to develop our thinking before we jump in with inadequate answers.

Leadership

It's so crucial that we are led by people who are growing themselves, who have not stagnated. Discipleship and the development of the Christian mind are a life-long journey. A leader who is learning is going to be enthused, energised and encouraged. We can create a church culture where this is affirmed rather than denigrated. We can get rid of anti-intellectualism and replace it with a passion for excellence in Christian teaching and thinking. We can buy our leaders stimulating books, send them on conferences or summer schools, we can encourage them to grow and to go on in this whole area of the mind. We can encourage them in their preaching, so that if we learn something new or are impacted by one of their talks, we cheer them on to keep them going on.

Chapter 5

Deep Character (1)

Many people who have been in church for a while, find themselves wanting to escape from any Christian expression which is shallow, limited to the surface or fake. This is a desire for authenticity. We believe that a crucial outworking of this sense is the development of Christian character. Now we need to be clear that what we mean by 'character' is not the same as 'personality'. Character takes place within a moral framework over-seen by God, whereas personality is a level playing-field, even though both are to do with the self and our relationship to others in society. Character can be good or bad, whereas personality is introvert or extrovert, without moral judgement.

The church and Western society in general have moved quickly from speaking in terms of character, to understanding the self in terms of personality, and they are poorer for it. The words and virtues associated with *character*, such as honour, duty, courage, moral integrity, gentleness and valour, were all sustained by a belief in a higher moral law, whereas the adjectives one would use to describe *personality* would include fascinating, stunning, attractive, magnetic, glowing, masterful, creative, dominant, forceful. David Wells writes:

None of these words could easily be used to describe somebody's character. Attention was shifting from the moral virtues which need to be cultivated, to the image, which needs to be fashioned. It was a shift away from the invisible moral intentions toward the attempt to make ourselves appealing to others, away from what we actually are and toward refining our performance before a public that mostly judges the exterior. The self-sacrifice of the older understanding made way for the self-realisation of the new. Now, it became important to find one's self, to stand out in the crowd, to be unique, to be confident, and to be able to project one's self.[1]

It is often failures of leadership and poor character within the church which make it into the media, and so we can easily gain the impression that the church is full of fakes and hypocrites. We were recently ministering in the States, in Colorado, when the head of the National Association of Evangelicals for America, who lived in the town we were visiting, was exposed in the press for drug-taking and a sexual relationship with a young guy. This man was a respected national church leader who was also somebody's husband and somebody's father. It was devastating to see the story unfold, to the glee of the newspapers. There are, unfortunately, plenty of examples of moral failings and poor character that we can bring to mind within the people of God.

Yet we are also aware of people with wonderful Christ-like, Jesus-like character. This is not an issue of personality – some will be wild at heart, others will be more retiring and peaceful. It is our experience that personality and character can easily become confused. Sometimes the articulate, beautiful, up-front or outwardly gifted individuals are assumed by leaders to be strong Christians. This is a dangerous assumption.

However, it can also be the case that in an effort to correct past mistakes, outgoing, young, attractive or achiever types can be assumed to be 'proud' because they are gifted. It is dangerous to assume that because someone excels they must have poor character. Christian character transcends personality, achievement, appearance, talent or the lack of any of these gifts. Christian character is rarely truly seen because it is, by its very nature, hidden to first inspection. It is the inner heart attitude. This will eventually come through, but it is not always immediately apparent.

It is also possible to spiritualise poor character, to hide our failings behind our schemes and slogans. Christ-like character gives the embrace of Jesus to all. But we can easily dress up our poor character issues by calling them other things. For example, 'My ministry is to people like myself', so I won't put myself in the uncomfortable position of living somewhere difficult and different, or even of talking and giving to people who are different. We may think: 'My ministry is to middle-class people who have got life together and are going to make excellent tithers to the body of Christ in years to come.' But this is just dressing our own selfishness up as spirituality, or embracing some principle of homogenous mission to make our own lives and church experience more comfortable. The New Testament vision of church is nothing like this. The New Testament envisions a church in which the haves and have-nots are worshipping together, where no worldly barriers of class, ethnicity, education or economic circumstance mean a jot, where no one is treated differently in church because of their financial or social position in the world. This is a very basic truth and yet we constantly come across wealthy people in positions of power in churches who would not be listened to in the same way if their background or financial situation were different.

What are the issues of character in our lives which we need the Holy Spirit to put His finger on? Issues of anger, or selfishness, or cowardice, issues of unclean language or thoughts, jealousy, pride, materialism? However, we want to avoid perceiving issues of character merely in terms of negative things – the vices, the things that we know we have to give up. We too seldom look at the virtues, the things that we need to build up in our inner lives, be they courage, service, generosity, kindness, faithfulness – Kingdom virtues which cause our hearts to rise and hope, which rub off on us from spending time with Christ.

Although some of us may feel disheartened at the state of the church in our nation today, things have been worse before, even in this country. J.C. Ryle, who was the Bishop of Liverpool, wrote about the state of the church and Christianity in England in the early 1700s in a book called *Leaders of the Eighteenth Century*. He described life before the revivals of Wesley and Whitfield, and the Welsh and Cornish Revivals:

> Christianity seemed to lie as one dead, in so much as you might have said, 'she is dead'. Morality, however much exalted in pulpits, was thoroughly trampled in the streets. There was darkness in high places and darkness in low places, darkness in the court and the camp, and parliament and the bar, darkness in the country and darkness in the town, darkness amongst the rich, and darkness amongst the poor – a gross, thick, religious and moral darkness, a darkness that might be felt.[2]

The state of this country, from a religious and moral point of view, was so painfully unsatisfactory that it is difficult to convey an adequate idea of it:

English people of the present day, who have never been led to enquire into the subject will have no conception of the darkness that prevailed from the year 1700 until about the era of the French Revolution. England seemed barren of all that is really good. The vast majority of the clergy were sunk in worldliness and they neither knew nor cared anything about their profession. They neither did good themselves, nor liked anybody else to do it for them. They hunted, they shot, they farmed, they swore, they drank, they gambled. They seemed determined to know everything *except* Jesus Christ and Him crucified. And when they preached, their sermons were so unspeakably and indescribably bad, that it is comforting to reflect that they were generally preached to empty pews.[3]

Ryle goes on to describe how the Archbishop of Canterbury had to be asked by the King to stop holding debauched parties and balls in Lambeth Palace.

Worship

The inner life – our thoughts, feelings, priorities, giving and life choices – forms part of our worship to God. In his book *The Living Church* John Stott comments:

The kind of worship which is pleasing to God has one more major characteristic. True worship is moral worship. That is to say it must not only express what is in our hearts, but also be accompanied by an upright life. Samuel put this beyond doubt in his explicit words to King Saul: to obey is better than sacrifice and to heed is better than the fat of rams.[4]

So what this is saying is that when we worship and we think about our worship with regard to our Christian character, our obedience to God is an act of worship. Choosing to obey Him and to follow Him, choosing to live a morally upright life that pleases God, is to worship Him.

One of our favourite writers is Alexander Solzhenitsyn, who was imprisoned under Stalin. He was put into a concentration camp for writing poetry, and while he was there, he observed some Christians who had been imprisoned for their faith, and he watched two Christian pastors being beaten to death by the guards. The way they died for their faith absolutely stunned him, so much so that he decided to become a follower of Jesus himself. After becoming a Christian, he wrote:

> If only there were some evil people somewhere, insidiously committing evil deeds, and it were necessary only to separate them off from the rest of us. But the line dividing good and evil cuts through every human heart.[5]

There is no pretence here – just a powerful, searingly honest look into the heart. If we want to worship God deeply and we want our character to grow and develop, we need to engage with this moral worship.

The word

How do we let God's word shape and challenge our character? We have some very good friends who are Iranian Christians, and one of these friends is quite a large man. One day his family were ribbing him about being a little bit overweight and telling him he needed to do some exercise. He is a really godly man who loves the word – he's a passionate Christian.

To their amazement, he said to his family, 'I don't believe in physical exercise. I think it's unbiblical.'

So his family said, 'Oh come on, what are you talking about? You need to get out and go jogging.'

He said, 'You know, jogging in particular is unbiblical.'

So they asked him, 'What do you mean?'

He replied, 'Well, Proverbs 28:1 says, "Only the wicked run when no one is chasing them." I've decided to apply the word of God to my life!'

But what does it mean practically to bring our character under the word of God so that we don't stagnate as Christians? Perhaps we think, 'I used to get drunk, I used to swear, I used to steal office supplies. I don't do that any more. Now I tithe my income, I stay faithful to my husband or wife, and I try to be a basically decent Christian. But now I'm going to stagnate, I'm going to stay here.'

No, rather than that, we should pursue deep godliness, so that even if we become a Christian as a teenager or as a child, and by God's grace we are given three score years and ten, throughout our life we can go on in Jesus, in character. We want to suggest that you should pray the words of the Bible for ourselves.

If you read Proverbs 3 as an example, you will read: 'My son, do not forget my teaching but keep my commands in your heart, for they will prolong your life for many years and bring you prosperity.' We could then pray that verse over our lives: 'Lord, I want your teaching. Please may your word be in my heart. Jesus, will you bring your word to my heart, will you bring areas of my life to my attention that need to come under your word?'

Proverbs 3 goes on: 'Let love and faithfulness never leave you. Bind them around your neck and write them on the tablet of your heart.' We could pray along these lines: 'Lord God, I want to move on in love; help me to move forward in faithfulness.'

Proverbs goes on: 'Then you will win favour and a good name in the sight of God. Trust in the Lord with all your heart and lean not on your own understanding.' This famous verse, when turned into a prayer, could become: 'Lord Jesus, I want to know your wisdom, your truth for the different situations that I face in my life. I don't just want to rest back on my common sense. Help me to lean on you. Jesus, I want to trust you. Help me do that.'

The passage goes on: 'In all your ways acknowledge him, and he will make your path straight.' Maybe there are some of us who need to start acknowledging God in the workplace or in His work that He has been doing through us, but we've been taking the credit for it. We bring our character under the word of God and pray God's word over our character.

Here's the verse that church leaders love: 'Honour the Lord with your wealth, with the firstfruits of all your crops, then your barns will be filled to overflowing and your vats will brim over with new wine.' Maybe we need to hear that – perhaps money has taken a hold in our lives, and we never thought of ourselves as particularly materialistic. We never imagined that once we reached 30, 40 or 50, really we'd have landed up basically living for a suburban dream or an ideal of comfort. God wants us to bring that area of our character under His word. 'Honour God with your wealth.' Honour God with your money – Jesus, help us do this. Praying the Scriptures over our character daily will produce the fruit of the Holy Spirit in our lives.

History

One of the things about character is that no matter what happens in any generation, the human heart is the same. This is why, if we want to go deeper with God, we can be inspired through history. Therefore the struggles of the great men and women of the past are relevant to us, so that reading their journals or biographies, we can learn so much. We can see what a reflected Christ-like character looks like – it can become a mirror for our own souls. Reading missionary biographies has shaped us both in terms of our strategy and mission activity and in our personal walks with God. Particularly helpful are the people who are honest about their failings, but who you can see visibly being transformed through the character of Christ. Amy Carmichael was a wonderful example of this – tenderly honest about her thoughts and failings, she established a ministry amongst children in India whom she rescued from temple prostitution and destitution. Character formation has been necessary in every generation, and so it is seen in exciting stories of God dramatically at work. Oswald Chambers' *My Utmost for His Highest* has been a mainstay devotional book in the lives of many wonderful Christians.

Richard Wurmbrandt was a Romanian church leader who suffered horrifically under communism. In 1966 he testified before the US Senate's internal security subcommittee, and was stripped to the waist to show scars – eighteen deep torture wounds covering his body. The story was carried across the world. He warned that he had a death threat against him. The book which tells his story, *Tortured for Christ*, commends the Christian virtues of courage, selfless love and sacrifice. We see the Christian character, not only of Wurmbrandt himself but also of many fellow Christians who were persecuted during the communist regime in the 1960s.

Isabel Kuhn's inspiring book *By Searching* talks about what she was learning about the Spirit of God and her character before going out to the mission field in China, where she worked amongst the Lisu people. She started Bible studies in the rainy season when nobody could plough their fields. Isabel tells the story of the awakening to the gospel amongst this tribe, but she also writes poignantly about juggling the anointing, the power, and the sense of experience of the Holy Spirit, and also the work of character. She touches on the fact that sometimes we can experience the Holy Spirit but our character remains unchanged, and she explores how to move beyond this. She writes:

> I always felt that there was a peril in just seeking an experience from the Lord. The temptation is to think that the experience has sanctified us, but it hasn't. These uplifting times in His presence, provings of His faithful care, they enrich us, they add to our joy but they don't sanctify us, they don't always make us stronger Christians, they don't make us holier than our fellows as I was to learn to my shame. But they do make us richer in our knowledge of Him, and they do give us a joy that is added to us with no sorrow in it at all. The only way to be holy is to daily hand over to the Holy Spirit what Dr Tozer calls 'the hyphenated sins of the human spirit': self-righteousness, self-pity, self-confidence, self-admiration and self-love and a host of others like them. They can only be removed in spiritual experience, never by mere instruction. We might as well instruct leprosy out of our system. There must be a work of God in destruction before we are free. We must invite the cross to do its deadly work within us. We must bring our self-sins to the cross for judgement.

Very often it's in the hard grind that the issue of character comes up. David Brainerd was a pioneer missionary amongst the Native Americans. His journals and diaries were said to affect people more than any other writing for over 150 years, as he passionately pursued prayer, wanting to see the Native Americans hear the gospel for the first time. He also details the intense struggles that he had on his journey. As you read these, you begin to see that suffering and perseverance produce character, that you can't get to character without the experience of suffering. Seeing this in the lives of others gives us hope, that as we suffer through disappointments and struggles, these can have a redemptive purpose in our lives.

Chapter 6

Deep Character (2)

Seek to be made holier every day; pray, strive, wrestle for the Spirit, to make you like God. Be as much as you can with God. I declare to you that I had rather be one hour with God than a thousand with the sweetest society on earth or in heaven. All other joys are but streams; God is the fountain![1]

Robert Murray McCheyne

Action

What can we do to pursue deep character? We can begin with desire, wanting to grow and develop as Christians, following this with repentance, by turning away from the things that we know are wrong. We can pray for our character growth through the Scriptures. We can be serious about growing as a Christian and not allow ourselves to be an adult baby. We make a baby step when we are born again; in the first couple of months we are still baby Christians. Our twin boys stumbled around when they were one, and at two played a game of pretending to be babies, crawling along on the floor and giggling as they became dirtier and dirtier. It was a great delight to see them do that and to watch them as they began to work out their lives and learn such things as the difference between kissing and biting! This is beautiful to watch, but we would be very upset if in married life they still didn't know the difference between kissing and biting! We would be very upset if they were still throwing themselves around on the ground and getting themselves all dirty just for the heck of it when they were 35. We are not to be adult babies in God's Kingdom. God's call for us is, of course, to be a child of God, but it is to grow into maturity and to repentance. Let us go on to maturity, to a deeper application of the Spirit's work in our lives – experiencing the gifts and the fullness of the Spirit but also actively pursuing the fruits of the Spirit.

Hospitality is a fantastic example of an action that we can take, which also works on our character. We open up our homes, we invite people in. It's one of the things we've seen in other church leaders, and so we want to do that ourselves. It can be exhausting to host and feed groups of people several times a week, but we truly enjoy spending time with people, and we know that our characters develop as we serve in this way. It's an action and a choice.

The end of the book of Proverbs is one of the places where we see a description of what a godly character is like. This example is a wife, but we can all take the principles of character within it seriously. Proverbs 31 says:

A wife of noble character, who can find? She is worth far more than rubies. Her husband has full confidence in her, she lacks nothing of value. She brings him good and not harm all the days of her life. She selects wool and flax and works with eager hands. She is like the merchant ships bringing her food from afar. She gets up while it is still dark and provides food for her families and portions for her servant girls. She considers a field and she buys it. Out of her earnings she plants a vineyard.

You may have noticed that this woman isn't your classic, typical stereotype of a Christian woman. Where's the bit about never going out to work? Where does it say you must always wear frumpy clothes and open-toed sandals? In fact, what we have here is an amazing affirmation in Scripture of a high-achieving woman, and the Bible characterises her as precious – she has high value, she works hard. Notice all the verbs in this passage – she is full of energy. The woman is described as working, bringing, getting up early, providing – she sounds like a whirlwind of activity.

> She sets about her work vigorously. Her arms are strong for her tasks. She sees that her trading is profitable, and her lamp doesn't go out at night. In her hands she holds the distaff and grasps the spindle with her fingers. She opens her arms to the poor, she extends her hands to the needy, and when it snows, she has no fear for her household, for all of them are clothed in scarlet.

This woman has sticking power and faithfulness, her business acumen is evident, her trading is profitable, she invests in property, she provides for others, for her family, and for her employees, she is creating wealth for others. This woman even has good arms! Yet she's more than a successful entrepreneur. She cares for the poor in her community, showing charity to people who need it. She cares for her children and her husband and she makes sure everybody has more than they need:

> She makes coverings for her beds, she's clothed in fine linen and purple. Her husband is respected at the city gate

where he takes his seat among the elders of the land. She makes linen garments and sells them and supplies the merchants with sashes. She's clothed with strength and dignity and she can laugh at the days to come. She speaks with wisdom and faithful instruction is on her tongue.

This woman has nice bed-linen! She's able to laugh at the future, rather than fearing it, she has authority in her home and is respected, she speaks wisely and knowledgeably about the word of God, teaching others what she has learned, she is full of joy and is able to encourage those around her.

The Bible isn't implying that we can become like this woman, someone who has a good character, by sitting around. Hard work is involved. This is a challenge for us. The Bible says that God's forgiveness of us is totally free, it is grace. His anointing of us for ministry, His giving of spiritual gifts, is all totally free. We don't deserve it. If we have a prophetic gift or a preaching gift or a gift of evangelism, it isn't because we've deserved it – they are all from the Holy Spirit. But when it comes to the issue of character and godliness, we are to be involved. It takes decision and effort on our part, co-operating with the Holy Spirit. The standards of this woman may seem unachievably high. But she isn't in the Bible to make us feel bad about ourselves, she's there to hold up an example to us, both men and women, that we can be people of character, of vocation, of passion and of energy. We can look after our families well *and* pursue God's Kingdom passionately. The two do not have to be mutually exclusive. We can work hard at our jobs in our vocational life and be successful at that, and pursue godliness, and character, and his Kingdom, and our families. We can fully enter in, with God's empowering and blessing, into a life of service and character for Him.

Mission

In evangelism our character speaks volumes, and it's amazing how often an evangelistic situation reveals what's really in our hearts. We have a friend who is Iranian, and he told us a wonderful story of a situation in Iran which happened soon after a number of Iranian church leaders had been martyred for their faith.

A couple who were friends of his were driving through central Iran from one meeting to another, and they had felt that God wanted them to speak to people every day about Jesus. So everywhere they went in their car, they had Bibles to give away to people. On this journey it was getting late and they drove up to a petrol station to refill their tank.

The husband was about to get out of the car when his wife said, 'Look, darling, go and speak to that man there.' She pointed to a man who was standing next to the place where customers paid for their petrol. He was clearly an Islamic fundamentalist – he was dressed in that way, and he had a gun with him. It was obvious that this was a tough call.

So the husband said, 'Thanks, darling, but you know, I don't really feel the Holy Spirit's leading me to talk to him.' And he shut the door of the car and went in and paid for the petrol.

As he got back into the car and drove off, they had a discussion that went something like this:

'You didn't speak to him, did you?'

'I didn't feel led; the Spirit wasn't drawing me to talk to him. I just didn't feel it was quite the right moment.'

So the wife said, 'Darling, when we stand before Jesus on the day of judgement and that man doesn't go to heaven, I will say to Jesus, "I wanted to tell him about you but my husband wouldn't let me."'

The husband started shouting and throwing his arms around in the air. 'Turn the car around!' he said.

They put the accelerator on and drove back to the place, and as he got out of the car and slammed the door, he left with the immortal parting words, 'If you want a martyr for a husband, you can have one!'

He went up to speak to the man. As he started to talk to him, this man began to cry. And as the husband produced a Bible to give to him, this hardened extremist had tears flowing down his face.

He said, 'Three days ago I had a dream, and in that dream, an angel appeared to me and told me to come here and wait, and that someone would give me the book of life. I've been waiting for two days. Thank you so much for stopping!'

There and then, our friend's friend led that man to faith in Christ. You can imagine the conversation in the car after that!

Character speaks volumes in mission. Even when we mess up, even when we nearly fail, God can still use it. Courage, faithfulness, kindness – all the Christian virtues in our lives point to Christ. In our area of Peckham we have a number of outreaches, and one of them happens in a bus on one of our estates. There's a guy from our church who is a human rights international lawyer, and once a week he gets home early from work and goes straight to that bus. His faithfulness to Christ is a beautiful thing.

A number of years ago our friend Simon Ponsonby, whom we worked with in Oxford, was walking in the University Parks with his dog, a chocolate Labrador called Caleb. He bumped into an American student, and they fell into conversation, initially about dogs, but they ended up talking about Jesus. This guy had come to Oxford to study and he was a very arrogant atheist.

When he found out that Simon was a vicar, he started laying into him about how there are no reasons to believe, and that since God doesn't exist, only stupid people believe in Him.

Simon began to ask him a little bit about his work, and he said, 'Well, I'm here because I'm so intelligent' (he had a big opinion of himself!). 'I've come here to study artificial intelligence under the world's leading mind in this area – that's how good I am.'

So Simon said to him, 'Oh, is that . . .?' And he named the leading person at Oxford in this field.

The guy looked amazed and said, 'How did you know?'

Simon said, 'Oh, he teaches children in Sunday School at our church!'

Now that was an amazing opportunity for the gospel, obviously, but it was character speaking volumes, because here was this revered person, giving their time to teach the children about the Bible.

Leadership

We explored the idea earlier that we can often look for personality, and we forget to look for character. At other times we think that the two can't come together. We are in a situation in our country where many of the people who are called leaders in our churches don't seem to be those who shine with the moral purity of our Saviour. And we want to be the kind of people who have Christ-like character, whatever our situation. We can encourage our leaders when we see them serving and working hard. When we have the job of raising up new leaders, we can look for character. Will they be people who help with the washing up as well as wanting up-front exposure? Are they the people who make it their job to sit next to the people we don't want to sit next to? Do they have sticking power – or do they give up easily? Maybe they're future leaders with real character. Character, in the hands of God, is worth more than anointing. We've become so personality and celebrity obsessed that we've forgotten that character comes before gifting, before personality, and even before anointing. God can give an anointing in the flash of an eye. Good and godly character takes time and work and perseverance.

A wife was making some scrambled eggs for breakfast one morning. Her husband came into the kitchen and sharply commented, 'More salt, more salt!'

She thought, 'Oh my goodness! OK, I'll put in a little bit more salt.'

He continued: 'More pepper, more pepper!'

She thought, 'OK, I'll put in more pepper.'

'Turn up the heat! Turn down the heat!'

So she said, 'Look, we've been married for twenty years, darling. Don't you think I know now how to make scrambled eggs?'

He said, 'I just wanted you to know how it feels when I'm driving the car – that's all.'

Perhaps we have fallen into habits of unhealthy criticism of leaders in the church, and we assume that they don't know what they are doing, and that we could do a much better job. And though we ought to expect much of our leaders, it is almost always better to pray than to nag, and better to examine our own failings than those of our leaders. They will be more open, trusting and likely to take your advice if they think you are fully supportive of them, their abilities and their calling.

Chapter 7

Deeply Physical (1)

The night before we were due to deliver this chapter as a message at the New Wine conference, one of our twin baby boys was given a nut. He ate it, and it got stuck in his throat, so Frog had to pick him up and run through the campsite, carrying our Elijah to the medical centre. I (Amy) followed behind with our other son, Zachary, who was completely oblivious to the drama which was unfolding.

Elijah couldn't talk, and he was really struggling to breathe. The medical centre staff were amazing. The nut had come out when we had patted his back, but we did not know if he was having an anaphylactic shock or whether his difficulty in breathing and talking was because something had been obstructing his air passage.

He was about to be given a shot of adrenalin, as he was not responding enough to the oxygen, and one of us said, 'Let's just pray now – we're going to pray in the name of Jesus!' And so we laid hands on our baby boy, and we prayed.

Now he hadn't said a word for forty minutes, although he'd been trying to talk but he just couldn't speak because his throat was so stuck. But as we said 'Amen' at the end of the prayer, he looked at the doctor who had laid hands on him with us, and she had a picture of a car on her T-shirt. Elijah pointed up and with great solemnity said 'Car!' No adrenaline was needed, nor any nights in hospital with him.

This terrifying, very physical experience dramatically brought home to us what we are exploring together in this chapter about the body.

Worship

One of the amazing things about the Christian message is that we worship a God who enters the space-time continuum. He is born into the world that He has created, in a real human body. Now as Christians we may be very familiar with this idea, but to the Greek world, the culture and context into which the New Testament was written, this was an astounding idea. The Greeks had a concept of a dualism of the life of the body and that of the spirit. They associated anything physical as being necessarily on a lower level than anything associated with God, which was a higher level, a spiritual plain untouched and unimpaired by anything grubby or physical. The physical and the spiritual were seen as being diametrically opposed to one another. To try to hold the two together was absolutely crazy. So when Jesus comes as God and enters our world, holding together the physical and the spiritual, the divine and the human, this was absolutely revolutionary. This is crucially important, then, since this idea is not held by the predominating host culture of the early church – it is a radically counter-cultural revelation.

Throughout the Bible, in both the New and the Old Testaments, we see that spirituality is integrally physical. In worship all kinds of physical imagery are used. In

Exodus 15:20 we see the first female worship leader in the Bible, Miriam. 'Miriam the prophetess, Aaron's sister, took a tambourine in her hand and all the women followed her with more tambourines and dancing, and Miriam sang to them.' This is an amazingly physical image of worship. A worship leader is singing – powerfully projecting her voice, playing a musical instrument and dancing. What a challenge to us – to develop the physical side of our worship and to develop our singing along the lines of this biblical norm. We are to sing, and sing loudly! Ephesians 5:19 says: 'Speak to one another with psalms, hymns and spiritual songs. Sing and make music in your heart to the Lord, always giving thanks to God.' If you think 'I really can't sing', develop your singing, practise at it, get better. Learn how to enter into worship with your body.

Now the Psalms develop this for us some more. Psalm 134:2 says: 'Lift up your hands in the sanctuary and praise the Lord.' I don't know if you've ever brought a non-Christian to church and had the amusing experience of watching them watch other people worship. When we lived in Oxford, our next-door neighbours became fascinated with the gospel and we used to have amazingly intellectual conversations over the garden fence about such varied subjects as Hindu reincarnation and Jesus.

One day they decided they wanted to come to church, but they wanted to come on a Sunday when Frog was going to be preaching and I (Amy) was going to be leading worship – they wanted to see both of us in action. We kept on missing each other and so one Sunday they just turned up. I found it hilarious the next day to hear the wife describing her church experience to our other next-door neighbours.

She said, 'It was quite amazing. We came in, and they had the words coming up on screens and a band started and we loved it. We both found ourselves crying inexplicably as we listened to the singing. We couldn't get over how loudly people were singing. All around us people were singing their hearts out.'

Then she saw me out of the corner of her eye and she said, 'Oh, I do have a suggestion for you. What you could do to improve the experience for people who aren't Christians is to have a sort of bouncing ball, like they have in karaoke, that goes along the words on the screens as you sing.'

Needless to say, we didn't take that particular suggestion on board!

Worship is a physical demonstration; to sing wholeheartedly requires some physical exertion. But why do we lift our hands? We do it because the Bible says when you come into the sanctuary, when you come into a place where people are praising and worshipping God, lift up your hands. This may seem like a strange thing to do – but even in Britain we see people raising their hands for their football or rugby team. But why do we do this? A useful analogy is the use of capital letters when typing something. If you are writing an email or a text message and put the 'Caps Lock' on, you use capitals because you're trying to emphasise what you're saying. This is what we do when we worship God and we want to put emphasis on the words that we're singing – we raise our hands up and we enter into worship with our bodies. The Bible strongly encourages us to do this when we worship God, as these physical acts are a demonstration to God of our desire to worship Him.

An interesting contrast is drawn in the Psalms between standing to worship with arms held high and sitting down. Psalm 137:1 says, 'By the rivers of Babylon we sat down and we wept and there on the poplars we hung our harps.' This is really interesting to us. We realised that in the Bible, when you sit down in worship, that is when you hang up your harp. When you get rid of the guitars and harps and music, you sit down to weep and mourn. But in contrast, you stand up and you lift up your hands and you dance to praise and to engage God. Added to these different physical postures, we also find these words in Psalm 138:2: 'I will bow down towards your holy temple.' We can bow down before God and demonstrate physically our humility before the Lord. We can also dance like David did, when he danced with all of his might. What a blessing that can be, to have men and women dancing with all of their strength. We have had the wonderful experience of being with the Ugandan church and finding ourselves in six-hour worship services, much of which involved loud intercession and enthusiastic dance during the singing – it was absolutely exhausting but brilliant!

A further physical expression of praise and worship is to shout. The Bible says that we should shout to the Lord to praise Him. 'Come, let us sing for joy to the LORD; let us shout aloud to the Rock of our salvation' (Ps. 95:1). Now, some of us are Anglicans, so we may not feel that shouting is appropriate in church on a Sunday morning; it may be that we need to go to a field, alone, and shout, so that people are not hindered by our worship, and so that you don't frighten any old ladies! It is incredibly releasing to shout out praise to the Lord with real enthusiasm. A lay leader from our church shared that he was recently slightly alarmed at the pre-service prayer meeting to see the vicar roaring a great big shout out before the Lord. Frog didn't realise there was anyone else there, and he was having a good old shout to the Lord! Learn how to shout, learn how to dance, learn how to lift up your hands, learn how to sit down when it's time to weep as well, learn how to sing and exalt the Lord, to sing loudly, to sing quietly, but to enter into worship with our bodies.

The word

There are five key things that the word of God tells us about the body:

1. Our bodies are precious

The Psalmist writes: 'For you created my inmost being; you knit me together in my mother's womb. I praise you because I am fearfully and wonderfully made' (Ps. 139:13–14). Our bodies are precious because they are the creation of God. We are made in His image and have essential worth and dignity because of this.

A number of years ago I (Frog) was spending a year teaching in a school in Johannesburg, South Africa. The head boy of the school at the time was a lad named Vusi. He was a wonderful Christian and he helped me set up a Christian Union in the school. He played the guitar and led worship, often taking moments to share with the other boys and girls about what Jesus had done for him.

One evening I started to ask him about his life, and it turned out that he was orphaned. When he was about 5 years old, he and his younger brother were left to live on the slag-heaps of the mines in Johannesburg. Many of these heaps are incredibly toxic and dangerous. After heavy rain they can just collapse, and mudslides sweep people away to their deaths. But he and his brother lived in that horrific place for several years.

One day, some nuns found them there and took them in, and they introduced Vusi to the Lord Jesus. He started to realise that he did have a father – a Father in heaven

– and that he was found and not lost. He began to develop his relationship with the Lord, and a sense of his own worth. I met him when he was 18. He had become an inspiring example of Christian character, though I don't know what he's doing now.

The preciousness of life is a doctrine taught by the Bible. The incarnation – Jesus becoming a human being – is an affirmation of every human body. Mother Theresa picked up children and the dying and has a home for the dying because life and flesh and bodies are precious. They may be temporary, but they are still precious. Those nuns picked up this boy Vusi because he was precious, even though for years he'd been neglected. The Bible tells us that we are made in the image of God and that we are precious.

2. We have a faith which is physical and spiritual at the same time

Our own following of the Lord is done in the body. Sometimes we are made all too aware of that through suffering. There are many different ways that this can happen. Sometimes when we're terribly over-tired, we find that we are not engaging with God in our quiet times. Have you ever found that if you're feeling distant from God, it coincides with exhaustion, and that by the end of a break or holiday things have completely turned around, and your quiet times are suddenly breaking through wonderfully and God is speaking to you? It is then that we remember that the body is important, and if we are tired and unalert generally, then it's much harder to be alert to God. A long-standing period of grief or unanswered prayer can have a similar effect. The death of someone close to us or a traumatic miscarriage has a physical impact upon us, and this affects us spiritually too.

Having had a long period of struggling to conceive and coping with miscarriage, we were overjoyed to welcome our twin boys Zachary and Elijah into the family. But when our boys were seven weeks old they were rushed into hospital with bronchialitis. Both of them needed to be in intensive care, but there were no beds available in London. We were offered a bed in France and one in Bristol, but the doctors felt it best not to move them in the end. By God's grace both boys pulled through and we could bring them home after a week in hospital. But we were on our knees with exhaustion, both physically and spiritually. We should not underestimate the impact of the reality that our faith is physical and spiritual at the same time.

One of the things that I (Frog) encountered at boarding school that made me work this through was being at the receiving end of very bad bullying. It began as a result of going along to the Christian Union. I found myself routinely beaten up every single Monday night after CU for about a year and a half. On one occasion I had been wounded so badly that I was sent to hospital, and I was then sent home for a week to recover. The day I came back to school, I was set upon by nine other boys and hit over the head with the heel of a shoe. My head was split open and I was sent to hospital again.

One of the problems I encountered at boarding school is that you are never safe. At two or three o'clock in the morning, some of the guys would get really drunk and they would come into my room and beat me up, and there was nothing I could do about it. I couldn't run home; I couldn't escape.

On another occasion a boy came into my room and said, 'I want to fight you.'

And I said, 'I don't want to fight. I'm a Christian – I don't do that kind of thing.'

And he said, 'I want to fight you now. I'll make you fight me!'

And I said, 'No you won't.'

So then he started insulting me, my mother, my dog and generally trying to rile me and provoke me. I was praying through this under my breath, and I had this moment of knowing that my physical life and my spiritual life had to come together here. I started to pray inwardly in my spirit. I'd received the gift of praying in tongues and I was just doing that under my breath at the time.

And he said, 'Fight me, fight me!'

I said 'No!' and he came up and he started to slap me round the face to get me to fight him, and he started to punch me, and then pummel me with all the power that he had in him, just laying blows into my back and my body and my legs and my arms, for about five to ten minutes.

I had an amazing moment there in the midst of that, when I thought this is where the physical and the spiritual overlap, but also where one takes over after the other. I thought to myself in my spirit, 'You can do what you like to my body, but Jesus has me with Him in the heavenly places and I'm seated at the right hand of God.'

It was my little experience of persecution – many other people face much worse things. But it has been a foundation for me in my life to overcome the fear of physical attack.

We have a deeply physical faith, but it is also deeply spiritual. We are seated with Christ in the heavenly places, we have been born again by the Spirit. He loves us and nothing can separate us from the love of God.

When we come to Jesus and give our life to Him, that union with Christ is real. It's not just a theological word. When the Bible says that we are in Christ, it is real. We really are with God in the heavenly places, and yet we are also here on Earth at the same time. It's one of those extraordinary mysteries.

3. The Word became flesh

Jesus affirms and inhabits the body in the incarnation. By entering the physical universe as a man, Jesus brings together the spiritual and the physical in the ultimate way. Graham Kendrick expressed this powerfully in this wonderful song (which was one of our favourites in our teenage years):

Meekness and majesty
Manhood and Deity
In perfect harmony
The Man who is God
Lord of eternity
Dwells in humanity
Kneels in humility
And washes our feet

O what a mystery
Meekness and majesty
Bow down and worship
For this is your God
This is your God

Father's pure radiance
Perfect in innocence
Yet learns obedience
To death on a cross

Suffering to give us life
Conquering through sacrifice
And as they crucify
Prays: 'Father forgive.'

Wisdom unsearchable
God the invisible
Love indestructible
In frailty appears
Lord of infinity
Stooping so tenderly
Lifts our humanity
To the heights of His throne

© *1986 Kingsway's Thankyou Music*

He embraces humanity and by becoming human lifts humanity to the very heights of Godhead.

4. The difference between the flesh and the spirit is defined for us in Scripture

Somebody may ask, 'How are the dead raised? With what kind of body will they come?' How foolish! What you sow doesn't come to life unless it dies. When you sow, you don't plant the body that will be but just a seed, perhaps of wheat or of something else. But God gives it a body as he has determined, and to each kind of seed he gives its own body. All flesh is not the same. Men have one kind of flesh; animals have another; birds have another and fish another. There are also heavenly bodies and earthly bodies; but the splendour of the heavenly bodies is one kind, and the splendour of the earthly bodies is another. The sun has one kind of splendour, the moon another, the stars another.

So will it be with the resurrection of the dead. The body that is sown is perishable, it is raised imperishable; it is

> sown in dishonour, it is raised in glory; it is sown in weakness, it is raised in power; it is sown a natural body, it is raised a spiritual body.
>
> 1 Corinthians 15:35–42

The 'flesh' here is the Greek word *sarx*. It means more than simply the human body. It means the body united with the human mind and emotions, tainted and broken by sin. That is the definition of the 'flesh'. A contrast is brought in this passage and in others between the flesh and the spirit. Not between the body and the spirit, which is the distinction that was made by Greek philosophy, particularly by the Platonists and the Neo-Platonists. The flesh, as described in Scripture, is the body, mind and emotions tainted and flawed by sin and decay and sickness and disease and the Fall. This is in opposition to the spirit, and the spirit is born in us when we are born again. That tussle, that battle, goes on in each and every one of us.

5. The word of God tells us of the resurrection of the body, and that all of us will be raised on the day of judgement

As Christians we believe that our body will be renewed and resurrected, not any more tainted by sin and disease and sickness and suffering. Jesus' resurrection body is a first-fruit of our promised resurrection. When Jesus was raised from the dead He was fully human, He was fully physical, He had the nail-marks in His hands, He had the wound in His side, He had the marks in His feet, and yet He was somehow changed. Doors were no longer a problem for Him. Jesus didn't cease to have a body.

But what does this affirmation by the Bible of the physical and the spiritual in the Christian life mean? It means that we as Christians say no to self-harm and the hatred of the body; instead we recognise that the body God has given us is precious. We disobey God when we look at ourselves and hate ourselves. Or maybe things are the other way around, and we have an obsession with looks, wanting to be beautiful all the time. This is challenged by the fact that our body will die and that we will be raised up and judged as to how we have lived. It also means that we say no as Christians to treating people differently based on their looks, either showing preferential treatment due to their good looks or degrading treatment for their bad looks. It means that we don't choose to go out with somebody or to marry somebody merely because of their looks. It means that as Christians we care passionately about the living conditions of our fellow humans and we act to right the wrongs that are done to people made in God's image.

I (Frog) once had the privilege of going to a small school in the countryside around Uganda, and in this particular area of Uganda the people thought that if somebody was disabled, there was an evil influence in that family. Since it was a shame culture, this meant that none of the other children would be able to get married if somebody in their family was disabled.

We met a local Christian who was the leader of the school, and he felt that it was his call under God to go and find all the disabled children in his area. Now why would that be a problem? Because the people hid their disabled children behind closed doors. He was often able to find these children and he would educate them in the school and look after them in the name of Jesus.

One day he was visiting a village, and he heard the sound of wailing and crying, and he discovered a small boy, who was about 7 years old. He found the boy chained to a wall. On the floor by him was a bowl of water and a bowl of food. His body was L-shaped – from the hips he just suddenly went out to the side. He had no power of speech because nobody had spoken to him for seven years. He was treated like an animal by many people in the family. They didn't want to kill him – they knew that was wrong – but they didn't want to treat him as a human either. They had kept him secret so that they could get their daughters married.

This Christian pastor who'd set up the school welcomed this child. I met that child about three years later when I visited the school with a friend of mine called Barney. They said, 'Come in, come in! The children want to sing for you!' And we walked into a room filled with disabled children. We had supper with them and they sang a song, and then this little boy sang.

We asked, 'What's he singing?' as it was in the local language.

The teacher said, 'He's singing "I'm beautiful because Jesus loves me."'

This boy was filled with worship in the presence of Jesus. Barney and I were on our gap year and we were trying to be really macho – and we completely failed and wept!

The word says that our faith is physical as well as spiritual – these two cannot be disconnected. So a deep and true relationship with God will fully embrace the physicality of life.

Chapter 8

Deeply Physical (2)

The third, to chastise the flesh, that is, giving it sensible pain, which is given by wearing haircloth or cords or iron chains next to the flesh, by scourging or wounding oneself, and by other kinds of austerity. Note. What appears most suitable and most secure with regard to penance is that the pain should be sensible in the flesh and not enter within the bones, so that it give pain and not illness. For this it appears to be more suitable to scourge oneself with thin cords, which give pain exteriorly, rather than in another way which would cause notable illness within.

Ignatius Loyola[1]

The church has got this area of how to understand our physical bodies wrong so many times in so many different generations! People like Ignatius Loyola have risen up in the church and taught a theology of flagellation. His writing on the imagination may be wonderful in parts, but it is not so good on self-scourging! Other writers suggest applying metal spikes to the inside of your thighs to allow the blood to flow, to help you realise that you should mortify your flesh! It has been part of our shame in the Christian tradition that we have misunderstood the bodies that God has given us, and we have mutilated them in a tragic misreading of Scripture. In Britain as well, Pusey, Newman and others reintroduced some of these spiritual abuses in the late 1800s as part of the Oxford Movement, and we have seen them rise to public attention with the publication of books like *The Da Vinci Code*.

Of course, there are positive biblical disciplines for the body, such as fasting. The great revivalist John Wesley decided that it was right for him to give up tea for the rest of his life, which he then did. The Puritans, whose writings form a wonderful historical heritage for us as Evangelicals to enjoy, understood the importance of the spiritual disciplines. Even following the same references which led to misinterpretation by the likes of Ignatius Loyola (1 Cor. 9:27 and John 15:2), they saw self-denial as a training regime in which they chased after closer relationship and intimacy with God, and the resulting purification of their lives. John Owen wrote:

> And our Saviour tells us how his Father deals with every branch in him that beareth fruit, every true and living branch. 'He purgeth it, that it may bring forth more fruit.' He prunes it, and that not for a day or two, but whilst it is a branch in this world. And the apostle tells you what was his practice, 'I keep under my body, and bring it into subjection.'

Such an interest in the disciplines of the Christian life is emerging again in the church today. We need to avoid legalism, works and self-hatred, but embrace the work of the Holy Spirit in the inner life of the Christian.

At the end of my (Frog's) gap year, I realised that there was a link in my life between beer and behaving inappropriately towards females. It became clear to me as I was praying things through that God wanted to deal with the latter, and therefore I had to deal with the former. I realised that I couldn't trust myself in a party situation, and I used to drink very heavily as a young man. I decided to give up alcohol for a year, and it was amazing to see how the discipline of fasting actually worked in my life. So much changed. My family were more than a little worried that I had gone 'over the top', as a glass of wine together is such an essential part of normal interaction for us. But it was wonderful for me to experience how God can use those spiritual disciplines to purify us and to work on our character.

Another particular spiritual discipline we affirm at this stage is feasting and celebration. It is a discipline to feast as well as to fast, to celebrate as well as to mourn. As Christians we are those who create the opportunity for others to celebrate and feast. The hospitality, the inviting, the fun is a discipline of the Christian life that should be embraced in the church. This can also have a wonderful missionary impact. Every year in Peckham we have a celebration feast, an international evening, where we pile into the church hall in national dress and set out stalls of our 'food from home'. After supper we have songs and dances and poems and readings, celebrating the international diversity of the people of God. I have eaten okra soup from Nigeria, goat curry from the Caribbean, shortbread from Scotland and spiced peas from Japan. We have heard schoolgirl songs from Indonesia, worn kilts and saris, and joined in dances from Uganda. We try, we taste, we share, we celebrate – we grow spiritually through feasting in our love and appreciation for one another. This is who the body of Christ is. Theo Hobson has commented:

> Our Christian culture needs to cultivate an anarchic lightness, a lust for freedom, a celebratory spirit. It needs to

learn from the boom in festival culture . . . we yearn to join a crowd that is celebrating. . . . Christianity is meant to be religion of celebration.[2]

To practise one or many of the spiritual disciplines is a beautiful thing which brings pleasure to God and to others. The dreary stereotype of a disciplined Christian is of someone dutifully undertaking unpleasant tasks because they have to. But the opposite is the case. A Spirit-filled act of service can easily bring me to tears. The ladies who clean our church do it as an act of love. They don't have much money to give, but they gladly give in this way.

Spiritual discipline, forming good habits, takes time. Getting up early in the morning while it is still dark is a brutal thing to do! However, if you do it more often, it gets easier. Your body adjusts to the idea of doing it. One of my (Frog's) joys of the last few years at All Saints Peckham has been the weekly men's prayer breakfast. When we came to the church, I was told, 'Yes the previous vicar always used to be at the 6.15 a.m. men's prayer meeting every Wednesday.' I thought, 'Oh no! Early mornings and dreary prayer! How am I going to cope? But I've got to keep up. I'm the new vicar, I don't want to slack, so I'll get up and I'll go to this meeting every Wednesday.'

The first couple of breakfasts were quite hard work, I have to admit. But five years down the line, it's wonderful to get up early with about fifteen or twenty other guys from the church and to worship the Lord together, to seek his face, to pray and put things right at the beginning of the day. This prayer meeting has become one of the power-houses of the church in prayer, prophecy, leadership and standing in faith for financial or territorial breakthroughs. For many of us it has become an essential habit.

What are the habits we are forming in our lives and our churches?

A newly married couple got back from their honeymoon. When the alarm clock went off in the morning, the husband went down to the kitchen and prepared his wife's breakfast on a tray – a nice pot of tea, with toast and marmalade, complete with a flower in a little glass vase. As he entered the bedroom he said, 'Darling, here's your breakfast.'

The wife thought, 'My goodness, I hit the jackpot here! I've married a fantastic husband – this is what my married life is going to be like!' She said, 'Darling, thank you so much – you shouldn't have!'

And he said, 'Well, I've done this so that you know what I expect now every day. This is how you do it.'

Are our habits godly, joy-filled obedience, or are they legalistic drudgery? There is a big difference. It takes time to form habits, but forming the right ones is essential for the Christian life.

Action

Inspired by the example of Christians who have gone before us in history, there are three important actions that we can take. The first is to affirm the work and the service that others do in the body. This is really important because so often, we think of our spiritual life as being separate from the life of the body. But actually, engaging in the spiritual disciplines, engaging in serving God and one another, is a physical activity.

The second action that we can take is to get our work and rest balance right for the body. There is a creation mandate in Genesis that we work for six days and we rest on one day. One day in seven should be, God says, a day of rest. Implementing this in your life is an action that you can take to honour God with your body. Often people say to me (Amy), 'How do you fit everything in? How do you manage to work and help with the church and look after twins and write and practise hospitality – how do you do it?' Well, the answer for us is that it is a spiritual discipline to have one day off in seven. We don't ever have a weekend because of church ministry, but we do always have one day off. We must do this; the Bible is absolutely clear and it's crucial for us in our lives. All through my schooling and university days I practised this by keeping Sunday as a day of rest, never doing any academic work on a Sunday. My friends at university thought I was crazy not to work on the day before my finals were to start, and I remember staring at the ceiling in St Aldate's on that Sunday and feeling peaceful about not being at my desk. Eric Liddell famously refused to run an Olympic race on a Sunday, as for him it was a day of rest. We now have a day other than Sunday as our day of rest, but the principle still holds – one day off from our work each week is a biblical mandate.

The third area that we can take action in is the area of our sexuality. Now, we haven't referred much to sexuality, because often Christian teaching on the body is totally focused on this area. Many people in our own church have experienced the horror of sexual abuse or violence at the hands of family members or acquaintances. In Peckham these situations can be extreme. But whatever our difficulties – whether we are unhappily married, or single and wanting to be married, or struggling with our sexual orientation – God can break into our hopelessness. He is the one who draws near to the broken-hearted. We have seen the beauty of this truth. The enemy wants us to believe that we are stuck in bondage and that God never really deals with such deeply physical and emotional realties.

Mission

Engaging ourselves in mission is going to be physically tiring and demanding. The apostle Paul talks about his experience of ministry as 'pouring his life out as a drink offering'. This is a dramatic, graphic image of what it means to give yourself for others in the path of the Kingdom of God. The body is involved in mission and preaching. If you're involved and engaged in social action or in evangelism, it is going to be physically and emotionally tiring. Sometimes people come to us and confess that they find that working full time in mission is too hard – it is too physically and emotionally drain- ing. They find that they do not have any time or energy for leisure activities and miss having a weekend off each week. This is not necessarily a failure, but rather a sense that they are not cut out for leadership in this par- ticular kind of work. This can be disappointing, but it can also be wonderfully releasing as they find a differ- ent vocation, and serve in a different way. Mission, and particularly pioneering mission, is hugely demanding and will have a physical knock-on. We all need to be aware of that and understand that there is this dyn- amic going on.

There are also other physical challenges when we engage in mission. In our church in Peckham we do a lot of work with young people. About a year after we had arrived there, we had a group of young people who were on the way to coming to know the Lord. Some of them had made commitments, but there were still some huge discipleship issues. When the police complained to

Frog about the behaviour of this group, he explained that these were people who were on a journey to find God, and he asked the police not to take their behaviour as a reflection of Jesus.

One of the group's leaders came to Frog and said, 'Frog, we believe in Jesus and the resurrection and all of that, yeah?'

Frog said, 'Yes.'

'So we've decided we're going to rename our gang. We're going to be called The Christian Gangstas.'

So Frog looked a little bit worried. He paused, and then said, 'Right, OK. So what's going to be different about your gang because you're Christians?'

'Well, because we're Christians we're not going to have guns.'

Frog thought, 'Fantastic!'

Then the young man added, 'We're only going to have knives, 'cos you've got to protect yu'self, innit!'

That evening we joked at home about the discipleship progression from guns to knives to blunt implements, and then perhaps one day to no violence at all. A year later the gang tensions flared up again, and after some pleading with them and some pleading with God, we were able to convince them to resolve their dispute with a game of football in the Park instead. This discipleship journey was almost complete!

The life of the body is involved in discipleship. In Peckham, discipleship issues are often issues of the body. But what are the body issues in your mission, in your community? Perhaps, when people become Christians, they realise that they need to get married. We've had the joy of seeing people come to Christ who've been living together, and they decide that to honour God now, in their new-found faith, they want to get married. It's a wonderful, beautiful thing.

Leadership

What does it mean to honour God, to be deeply physical, as leaders? The first thing to do here is to revisit the whole area of rest. One of the great tragedies of Christian leadership is the tragedy of burnout. Some of us have seen leaders being shipwrecked through being overly busy. This is partly because church leaders often believe that other people believe that they only work on Sundays. And so we need to justify our existence, and so we work and work and work really hard, so that people can see that we're working, not just on Sundays. We all need to encourage our leaders to rest. Leaders reading this need to hear this word from God: you must be obedient to God's word and have at least one day of rest per week.

Another very simple thing is the whole area of holidays. Many Christian leaders earn relatively little – perhaps enough to make ends meet but not enough to enjoy a holiday away. This is an indictment of the church, and this is an area where we can learn from our African and American brothers and sisters. Generosity and love towards a leader pleases God. Worrying that they have it too easy or that they might become too well off is virtually always unnecessary in the UK. We had this wonderful experience in our church of a couple just offering to pay for us to go on holiday a few years ago, and it absolutely amazed us. It really was a restful break and we came back raring to go. If you can't afford a holiday, maybe you could pay for your leader to go out for a nice meal.

Physical tiredness actually affects us in how we hear from God and how we interact with people. We need to try to understand that leaders are human and may get tired. They need rest. They need allowances to be made for the physical challenges of what they're involved with. All leaders suffer at some time from discouragement and criticism – sometimes this can get to the point of physically overwhelming us.

Most people have job reviews at work these days – one on one with their boss, supervisor or line manager, perhaps twice a year. Those in leadership often have this process carried on without a structure, every other week, and in the public eye. Nehemiah 6 describes what a deep impact that can have. Nehemiah has only completed half the wall, but as he presses on with his building team, his neighbours get restless and start plotting against him. They send him messages privately, then publicly, finally sending an unsealed letter to him, suggesting that he is being rebellious:

> Sanballat and Geshem sent me this message: 'Come, let us meet together in one of the villages on the plain of Ono.' But they were scheming to harm me; so I sent messengers to them with this reply: 'I am carrying on a great project and cannot go down. Why should the work stop while I leave it and go down to you?' Four times they sent me the same message, and each time I gave them the same answer. Then, the fifth time, Sanballat sent his aide to me with the same message, and in his hand was an unsealed letter in which was written: 'It is reported among the nations – and Geshem says it is true – that you and the Jews are plotting to revolt, and therefore you are building the wall.'
>
> Nehemiah 6:2–6

I (Frog) was reading this passage in my devotions in early January 2008, and a few days later I received a letter suggesting that All Saints was acting illegally, and threatening to take us to ecclesiastical court over – you guessed it – a building issue! The church had been near derelict for years, but it was not the *ruins* but the *rebuilding* that brought us to the attention of the legal eagles. On the same day, a Christian magazine, which had previously published a warm article about the work we have been doing as a church in our community, now printed two letters from other Christian leaders in the area. We were apparently too white, and too Anglican, and too inexperienced, said one; and the other letter also carried a few barbs. I have an entirely supportive church council, which helps, but the experience left us both tired and drained, and a bit battered.

We talked in our church council meeting about this passage, and Nehemiah's responses spoke to our souls:

> so I sent him this reply: 'Nothing like what you are saying is happening; you are just making it up out of your head.' They were all trying to frighten us, thinking, 'Their hands will get too weak for the work, and it will not be completed.' But I prayed, 'Now strengthen my hands.'
>
> Nehemiah 6:8–9

Leaders need encouragement. The opposition can be so draining at times, spiritually and psychologically, that we need prayer just to keep going. We prayed that night for strengthened hands and the courage not to be diverted or distracted from the project God had called us to, and called us to finish!

Chapter 9

Deeply Immersed (1)

My (Amy's) father became a Christian in his thirties as a university lecturer, and after his conversion he felt that God was calling him into full-time Christian ministry to plant churches. So I grew up in the church. When, a few weeks after we had met, Frog slightly nervously said, 'I think God might be calling me to get ordained in the Church of England', I comforted myself with the thought that 'They'll never accept him – he's far too wacky!' But it happened.

Here are some notices which have appeared in church bulletin sheets:

Don't let worry kill you – let the church help.

On Thursday night there will be a bring-and-share supper. There will be prayer and medication afterwards.

At the evening service tonight, the sermon topic will be 'What is hell?' Come early and listen to the choir practice.

Weightwatchers will meet at 7 p.m. at the Central Baptist Church. Please use the large double doors at the side entrance.

Deirdre Williams is in hospital and is having trouble sleeping. She requests that someone bring her tapes of Pastor Paul's sermons to help.

The church is a funny place to be at times, but it's also a wonderful place to be. Bill Hybels made this famous statement: 'The local church is the hope of the world.'[1] We really believe that and have become increasingly convinced that evangelism and nurture need grounding, and that this needs to be in a local church community if the hidden people are to be found. Do you believe that 'the local church is the hope of the world'? Have you become convinced, as we have, that the transformation of society is best achieved through the transformation of individual human hearts brought into contact with their Maker and Redeemer?

Worship

As we explore together what this might mean to us as Deep Churches, we will be considering lots of questions: What does it mean to worship God, whilst being fully immersed in our community? Can we hold together being outreach-orientated and being worship-orientated? Can we hold together, on the one hand, being a light to our community, having a passion for those who don't know Christ to come in and find Him, and on the other hand, having a passion for worshipping Him?

In our first year at All Saints Peckham, the Lord did an extraordinary work of conversion, and a lot of people came to know the Lord Jesus – probably around a hundred, although we never counted them properly. The church just kept on growing at a phenomenal rate. We were joined by other Christians later, but at the beginning of our time there the vast majority of the growth was through conversions. This was largely through the work of our incredible team of evangelists ministering full time out in the community.

One of the people who had come along to the church at that time, through a friend, was involved in local politics, and he asked to meet with Frog to discuss where he was at. As they sat down together to have a beer, this man said, 'You know, I love and I hate All Saints.'

And Frog thought, 'Oh, this is going to be an interesting conversation!'

The man continued: 'I love coming to a place where all of the different groups in the community are gathered together. You know, there is nowhere else in Peckham, other than the church, where you have black and white, African and Caribbean, young and old, middle class and working class coming together. If you go to pubs, people just drink in a different pub. If you go down to a community centre, different mini-communities meet together. It's only in the church that they come together. I love that! If only you could just stop talking all the time about God and Jesus, I'd come every week! It would be brilliant.'

Now, of course, Frog said, 'It's only really because of God and Jesus that we can come together and be together.' To him, a worshipping community which was multicultural, multi-age and gathered across the social spectrum, coming together to worship God, was an amazing witness in the community. Here's a challenging question: 'Is our worship a witness in our community?'

A few years ago, when we were working in Oxford, our church had a baptism service for new Christians to be publicly baptised. A young man got up to give his testimony, to explain why he had become a Christian. As he was talking, the vicar asked him, 'Can you tell us a bit about why you want to be baptised?' He replied that, a year before, his wife became a Christian and he was absolutely furious. Everybody suddenly felt a bit nervous about what was going to happen next – you could feel the tension in the building.

He continued that he decided to convert her back to being a non-Christian. He worked out exactly what his strategy was going to be, and he bought a journal. His wife had started praying every day, so without telling her about the journal, he thought every day for a year he would ask her what she was praying for. In his journal he would write this down and have a page next to it to write down answers to prayer. He thought that at the end of the year, he would be able to give this book to his wife and say, 'Look at all these prayers you've prayed, and look at all the blank pages! God hasn't answered any of them. He isn't real. Go back to being a non-Christian.' In the church, you could feel the hostility rising towards this poor guy.

But he explained that what happened instead was that, after asking her what she had been praying for and writing it down, a few days, or a few weeks, or even a few months later, he found himself having to go back to that blank page and filling it in with the answers. And so instead of handing her a book filled with empty pages, he found himself holding a book filled with pages of answered prayers. The only unanswered prayer was for his own conversion to Christ, and that was soon answered too! He finished by saying, 'Here I am today to be baptised.'

Worship and prayer in the people of God can be the most amazing evangelistic tools. This is when the reality of God at work in our lives, at work in our church, can impact on those outside the church, and they can begin to see it. When people see this reality, some will be drawn to want to know more. There will be other people who say, 'Well, does God really exist? There's no evidence for his existence other than your experience.' This is where it is important for us as Christians to be able to put our experience of God into the broader context of the public evidence for His existence. There are many reasons that we can give people to believe in God, but five reasons stand out as useful pointers that we can give to friends who don't believe in God. We believe that this is actually part of our worship – to affirm His existence to others.

The cosmological reason

This is simply that the universe around us, of which we are a part, exists at all and is so complex that it points to the existence of a rational God who created that universe. The Psalms say this: 'The heavens declare the glory of God.'

The epistemological reason

Don't be put off by these long words – 'epistemology' just means the theory of knowing anything. The fact that there is knowledge at all and human beings can know things and communicate them suggests that there is a rational being who brought the universe into existence. So if you don't believe in God, you actually have no basis for thought at all. It's rather amazing, because atheists love to talk about knowledge all the time.

The moral reason

If God exists, then morality has an absolute location. Morality isn't just what you or I feel or make up as we go along the way as individuals, and it isn't merely what society decides. It is rooted, not arbitrarily in us, but in the being of God. If God exists, morality exists.

Richard Dawkins made the famous statement in one of his books that there is 'no design, no purpose, no evil and no good. Nothing but blind pitiless indifference. DNA neither knows nor cares, DNA just is and we dance to its music.' Dawkins was asked by a student, 'What about the Holocaust? Could you say that that was evil?' He answered, 'No. I can say I don't like it, but I can't say it was evil.' If we dispense with God from the picture, then our moral categories are purely arbitrary.

Now sometimes people say, 'OK, but that's why we have a legal system and our morality has evolved, and so communities have developed moral systems and some things are right or wrong within a community.' But if God does not exist, those systems are not absolute – they apply only within that community. (And this was exactly the defence that the SS used at the Nuremberg trials, to defend the Holocaust.)[2]

If God exists, there is someone who is a judge between good and evil in an absolute sense, not just arbitrarily what you or I think or what our nation or another nation happens to think.

Historical reasons

There is historical evidence surrounding the life, death and resurrection of Christ, as well as the evidence within the Bible for God's existence.

Personal reasons

This simply means that you and I have met and encountered God. He has changed us, we know that we know

Him, we have a relationship with Him. We can no more deny our relationship with God than we can with someone else. Now this isn't enough on its own to convince a sceptical person necessarily, but it's one of five arguments that you can use.

We can worship God by vouching for His existence in a community and nation that believes He is a total and complete irrelevance – that is to worship Him. To speak His name, to tell of Him, to defend Him, to present Him to others is to worship Him in our community. If we are to be deeply immersed as Christians, this is what we should be doing – speaking of Him and telling of Him.

The word

As we worship the God who is real, we take His word, the Bible, to a world that is totally and utterly sceptical. I (Amy) love listening to BBC Radio 4, even though it is frequently terribly sceptical about Christianity. A few years ago I was listening to a programme in which somebody was interviewing an archaeologist about his work in the desert, since they had recently discovered the city of Sheba – the same city from which the Queen of Sheba went to visit Solomon in the Bible.

The archaeologist was talking about this amazing find, and the interviewer was saying, 'No, no, no – what you are saying is, you think you've found some remains which *might* be Sheba.'

The archaeologist replied, 'No, actually we've found these huge, high walls, we've found inscriptions, we know that we have found Sheba.'

Then the interviewer said these words, which I will never forget: 'You aren't honestly trying to tell me that the Queen of Sheba is a historical figure?! She is, after all, a *biblical* character.'

In other words, if something is in the Bible, it must be fictitious.

In our communities, the word of God is either totally unknown, or is despised by many, and so if we are to be deeply immersed, we need to be those who take the word to the world. It was Leslie Newbigin who famously said that the gospel is 'public truth'. That means it isn't just true within our little community of the church, but it's actually *true* – or, as Francis Schaeffer said, 'This is true for the totality of reality.' The gospel isn't just true for 'religious' people – this is God's word applied to the whole of life and the whole of the world. We must take this truth to *heart*, then take it to the *streets*, and do it in such a way that it will be *heard*:

> But being personal does not mean that it is subjective. The faith is held with universal intent. It is held not as 'my personal opinion', but as the truth which is true for all. It must therefore be publicly affirmed, and opened to public interrogation and debate. Specifically, as the command of Jesus tells us, it is to be made known to all the nations, to all human communities of whatever race or creed or culture. It is public truth. We commend it to all people in the hope that, by the witness of the Holy Spirit in the hearts of others, it will come to be seen by them for themselves as the truth.
>
> Leslie Newbigin[3]

This is what motivated and informed the Apostle Paul as a missionary to the not-listening world, the world where there was no vacuum of belief waiting to be filled, but rather a world like our own where other ideas and powers seemed to govern the public spaces and the public debates. God's word to the Philippians therefore speaks to us as well: 'be blameless and pure children of God without fault in a crooked and depraved generation, in which you shine like stars in the universe as you hold out the word of life' (Phil. 2:15–16).

So how do we do this – how do we take God's word to the world? How do we get the Bible back onto the agenda of our communities? For us, one way of doing this is to start an evangelistic bookshop ministry, and this is mainly focused at reaching out to Muslims. We have called our bookshop 'Abdul Massih', which means 'servant of the Messiah'. (Abdul Massih was the first Islamic convert in India to become an Anglican minister.) Anyone who speaks Arabic knows what this name means. Our bookshop sets up on a Friday and Saturday as a stall in Peckham. It sells Bibles and literature in all the languages of those who live in our community. We need to be taking the word to the world.

We are also starting an initiative to make sure that every young person in our local schools in Peckham has their own Bible. This is something which previous generations in Britain could take for granted, but now it is rare to find a home with a Bible in it. So we are giving a Bible to every child who attends a local school, hoping to get the word of God not just into the hands, but into the homes of our community.

History

The church, deeply immersed in its community, is something that has happened through history, and particularly for the Evangelical churches. However, there has been a historical pattern of engagement followed by withdrawal. When Evangelicalism is in its ascendancy, social action always happens. This is how we saw an end to slavery in the British Empire, the introduction of clean water into the inner cities of Victorian London, anti-gambling campaigning and legislation, literacy for children, the end of child labour in factories, the banning of the use of children for chimney sweeps. It is well documented that all of these initiatives were inspired and led by Evangelical Christians such as Lord Shaftesbury and William Wilberforce, and that the Victorian inner cities were transformed through the likes of the Salvation Army and the London City Mission.

Evangelicals also tackled alcoholism in sometimes unusual ways. Guinness was developed by Arthur Guinness, who was a Christian man from God-fearing stock. At that time, alcohol abuse was a major social evil. Guinness invented his famous stout as a way of combating this problem. The stout was very good for you and so rich and heavy that it was very difficult to drink large quantities of it – thus making drunkenness unlikely![4]

What do we mean by 'Evangelical Christian'?

Evangelicals are those people who hold that the word of God is primary for understanding our traditions and our practice, our actions and our theology and our theory. We do develop, we do engage with the word of God and we interpret it afresh in every generation, but we have a check and balance to what we do in church and in the world, and that check and balance is the revealed word of God – the Bible. It is this that has an authority over and above my own understanding and the understanding of my leader and of the traditions or theologians around me. It is the word of God that is primary. It instructs my reason, it instructs my will, it instructs my emotions.

Another characteristic of an Evangelical is the central-
ity of the cross of Christ in our thinking. The cross of
Christ is not just a moral example for us to say, 'Oh look,
there is someone who's given up his life for his friends.'
Rather, something objectively happens at the cross, and
if we do not go there, we will not be saved. If we do not
accept what's happened at the cross, our sins are not forgiven. Objectively, God actually does something by
Christ dying on the cross and rising again.

The third defining thing is conversion. People need to
respond to Christ's offer of forgiveness and be born
again – or converted. Something real, something onto-
logical happens when we are converted, which has nothing to do with our human efforts and everything to do
with the very person and power of God entering our life,
forgiving us and transforming us from within. This new
birth has eternal implications – we are born again not
just for this life but for heaven. We are rescued from
punishment in hell for the wrong that we have done in
this life, and we are welcomed into heaven because of
what Christ has done.

A fourth element is mission – we have a calling, which
is to take the gospel to the world. This public truth, the
gospel which refers to the totality of reality, is true for
the entire universe. God is real, whether you believe in
him or not. Every person should have the opportunity to
personally respond to this, and so we take the message
out wherever we go.

The fifth element of what it means to be an
Evangelical is the active work of the Holy Spirit in the
life of the believer. The third person of the Trinity is filling the converted Christian, instructing, guiding,
empowering and sanctifying us. We are not alone.

These five aspects are historically what it has meant to
be an Evangelical, and they go right back to the very

roots, to Scripture itself and into church history. Where the word of God, the Bible, stands over us in all of our words and practices and doctrines and actions, and the cross is the centre of our faith, by which we interpret everything in the Old and New Testaments, and where being converted and accepting Christ for ourselves, and this mission, this activism, the work of the Spirit in the life of the believer – where we hold to those things, the transformation of society flows out. Always.

Evangelicals like Shaftesbury, Wilberforce and Booth genuinely transformed British society. This was because they had been instructed and convicted by the word of God and the work of the Spirit in them, that the suffering and injustice that they were seeing in front of their very eyes could not carry on without them throwing themselves into their community and becoming deeply immersed. They were driven by God to work in the slum dwellings in the towns and cities across the nation, and to seek the lost. Hudson Taylor said, 'I cannot sleep at night, when there are a billion people in China who have never heard the Gospel.' The Chinese Inland Mission was birthed out of that. The great 'Missionary Century' was also the Evangelical century, and it was also the century of social transformation.

The British politician and historian Roy Hattersley wrote:

The Salvation Army which William Booth founded – although sometimes derided as an essentially nineteenth-century organisation – can take pride in having helped ease Britain out of its nineteenth-century attitude to sin and poverty. It can also boast a million little miracles – wounded soldiers on the front line given tea and two-inch thick sandwiches; drunks sleeping under bridges persuaded to dry out, wash up, and look for work; girls escaping from tyrannical parents convinced that it is better to live under friendly supervision than in the unprotected custody of pimps. It is not necessary to believe in instant sanctification – or in sanctification in any form – to admire and applaud their work of social transformation.[5]

But what we see in our history is this cycle of engagement and retreat. When we as Christians hold to the truth of God as revealed in Christ and in His word, we are transformed and we transform society. But then people come along who like the effect, but they don't like the person of Christ, or the message about Him. They like the effects but not the Effecter. And so they want social action without Christ and His claims. They love what we are doing in the community, but want us not to proselytise. But if Christ is the whole reason that we're doing this social action, and we get rid of Him, we are left with mere niceness. Nice never changed the world. Nice doesn't save from sins. Nice doesn't give you eternal life. Nice doesn't cover our shame and our disgrace and our guilt and our fear. Nice doesn't deal with eternity and death. Nice doesn't rescue from hell. Jesus does. The gospel does. A deeply immersed church has the person of Christ and His gospel at the front of her presence in the community.

We want to give you a little image. Think of yourself as an arrow in the hands of God. Your point – the point of contact by which you become deeply immersed in the world in which God has put you – that point is encounter with God through the gospel. If you want to make an arrow fly quicker, you put oil on its head, and it goes in deeper. Think of that oil as the anointing of the Holy Spirit for you to get deeply immersed in your community, with the gospel as the point of that deep immersion. And the power of God draws that bowstring behind us and propels us to the lost and the dying and the broken. Being a deeply immersed church, a deeply immersed individual in our community, means that we are deeply impacting those around us. But the gospel is always at the forefront – at the arrow-point.

The Holy Spirit fills us, in part to equip us and motivate us for the call and cause of mission. This outward drive is motivated by love and freedom rather than guilt, and allows us as Christians to experience in prayer and in action the same love which beat in Jesus' own self-sacrificial heart. This verse from a missionary hymn expresses this very well:

O Father who sustained them
O Spirit who inspired
Saviour, whose love constrained them
To toil with zeal untired
From cowardice defend us
From lethargy awake!
Forth on Thine errands send us
To labour for Thy sake.

Lyrics by Frank Houghton, OMF

Indeed, after Jesus' own baptism of the Holy Spirit, He found himself being led *by the Spirit* into the wilderness and into preparation for ministry and the spiritual battle. It was by the Spirit that the signs and wonders, miracles, healings and raisings from the dead occurred, and it was the power of the Holy Spirit that raised Jesus Himself from the grave. So we should pray for more of the work of the Spirit in and through us.

Francis of Assisi is very often quoted as saying, 'Preach the gospel; if necessary use words.' As fans of Francis' ministry, it is astonishing to us how often this is repeated approvingly. It's highly doubtful whether

Francis ever said those words anyway, but one thing that's clear is that the word of God has priority even over the life of a great saint. If Jesus told us to preach the gospel and that we do need to use words, and if Jesus himself needed to use words to preach, why would we not use words to make the gospel known? The apostle Paul says, 'How can they know, without somebody telling them and preaching to them?'

In fact the extraordinary thing about Francis of Assisi, if we're going to look at him, is that he was marked out, from all of the other saints and leaders of his time, by his giftedness to preach the gospel and to heal the sick in Jesus' name – he used words a lot. He was a passionate and enthusiastic preacher.

He trained and equipped both laypeople and other monks to preach the gospel, so much so that if you go to the Franciscan Basilica in Assisi, you'll see pictures of Francis and his team going even to the Sultan and the Islamic world, preaching the gospel during the Crusades. Franciscan monks and preachers went to one side of the fighting armies and they preached the gospel to them, and many of them were converted. Then to the shock of all observers, they packed up their bags and went across the front line to the other side, where the Islamic armies were camped, and they preached exactly the same message to them.

Francis was so passionate about preaching and so gifted at it that a whole new form of building and painting had to be developed to cope with the response. They needed to build new churches that could take over 2,000 people sitting to hear the preached word. These buildings were huge, and they had to work out how to decorate them, so they came up with frescos. How else were you going to cover enormous walls and make them feel like a place of worship? They built these barns and then they filled them with people and colour. The art and architecture were a response to the preaching of the gospel.

How ironic that the very person who is quoted as saying, 'Go into all the world and preach the gospel; if necessary use words' was one of the best and most inspiring preachers of his generation, who transformed Italy and much of the known world through his ministry. The lessons of history should actually bring us back to being deeply immersed.

Throughout history there has been a pattern of Evangelical engagement and retraction. At the turn of the century a movement arose amongst Christians called the 'social gospel', which was trying to say that the church exists primarily to do good works and relieve material poverty, that preaching about Christ and His cross is no longer important or desirable. Of course, Evangelical Christians rejected this, but in so doing many lost sight of any engagement with the community in their efforts to maintain doctrinal purity within the churches. This battle over doctrine was crucial, since the social gospel movement arose alongside liberal theology, which was a movement based on 'demythologising' the Bible – which simply means explaining away any miraculous content, including the divinity of Christ. Liberal Christians were also denying the objective nature of Christ's atoning death, downgrading the cross from an actuality to an example.

It was in the 1960s, and particularly in 1967 at the Keele Evangelical Conference, that Evangelicals began to recapture a vision of being called to bring together these two elements – proclamation of the gospel and engagement with society – without losing one or the other. The possibility arose once again of being socially engaged and deeply immersed in our community, but

never neglecting the authority of the word of God and
the message that we have. This was reaffirmed in 1977
when Tearfund was launched. Tearfund stands for The
Evangelical Alliance Relief fund. The heart of this was to
say that we are not going to lose the gospel, and we are
not going to lose social engagement: we want both. This
is what it means to be deeply immersed: it means that
we want it all.

The Manila Manifesto, a document formulated by an
international group of evangelists and scholars in 1989,
puts the inseparable union this way:

> Evangelism is primary because our chief concern is with
> the gospel, that all people may have the opportunity to
> accept Jesus Christ as Lord and Saviour. Yet Jesus not only
> proclaimed the Kingdom of God, he also demonstrated its
> arrival by works of mercy and power. We are called today
> to a similar integration of words and deeds. In a spirit of
> humility we are to preach and teach, minister to the sick,
> feed the hungry, care for prisoners, help the disadvantaged
> and handicapped, and deliver the oppressed. While we
> acknowledge the diversity of spiritual gifts, callings and
> contexts, we also affirm that good news and good works
> are inseparable.

The next question, then, is: What is the history of your
community? What is the history of the local place in
which you are rooted and established, where your
church meets and worships? How did that worshipping
community start in the place where you worship?

When we arrived in Peckham we got very excited one
morning, having read together in our Bible readings the
story of King Josiah in 2 Chronicles 34. We found a whole
collection of papers whilst clearing out some skips filled
with rubbish. Now, of course, this was nowhere near as

exciting a discovery as Josiah's – he found the book of the Law! – but we came across a large metal trunk containing the archive of the church. An 'archive' is a generous description of it really – it was just a lot of papers all mixed together, dating from 1867, when the church was planted. We looked through them and discovered that the church had been planted by a guy called Thomas Gaster, who had been a missionary sent to India in 1856. When he returned to the UK he worked as a curate in a church in Camberwell, and then Holy Trinity Clapham. This is the church where the 'Clapham Sect' had worshipped, including William Wilberforce. This church had been instrumental in bringing transformation to the previous generation in Britain. Gaster went there at a time when the church was beginning to lose its way, and since he was such good preacher, it started to fill up again. The vicar at the time wasn't so keen on this, and a bit of tension developed between the incredibly popular, brilliant and dynamic curate and the vicar, who wasn't so popular. The solution was a church plant! Gaster was sent, and many of the congregation, who remembered the heart of the Clapham Sect, poured their money out, and that's how our church was founded. With a great missionary drive, Gaster was sent to this new area called Peckham, which had few churches. Back then, Peckham was a leafy suburb which was being filled up with unchurched people. The church met in Gaster's home and grew through a door-knocking ministry in 1867. By the end of that year, it had over 100 people, and within 4 years there were 400 adults in the congregation. They built a school to worship in, but they outgrew the school, so they built a church building – and the church has been in that place ever since.

Although the church has been through periods of stagnation, in its history there is so much to inspire us.

We have been expanding our children's and youth ministry, seeing unchurched young people come to Christ – and we were astonished to discover that this is what All Saints had done a hundred years before! When the Lord gave us a vision to transform our derelict church site, which had been completely devastated by seventy years of neglect, He gave us a verse from Isaiah 51: 'The Lord will surely comfort Zion and will look with compassion on all her ruins; he will make her deserts like Eden, her wastelands like the garden of the Lord. Joy and gladness will be found in her, thanksgiving and the sound of singing.' He gave us a vision of a singing, worshipping community in a transformed wasteland – a garden.

The church had no proper boundaries and the back of the site was overgrown with impenetrable weeds and trees. The land bordered the council car park and had become a main point for drug deals. This land has been completely transformed into a beautiful garden in which children and families can play, church groups can meet in summer months and wedding receptions can be held. God transformed our wasteland into a garden.

You can imagine how encouraged we were to later discover that when Gaster originally bought the plot of land for All Saints to be built – it was a beautiful garden! The church was built in a garden and God gave us a vision to restore that. These physical transformations are prophetic and practical. They are prophetic of what the Lord is doing in the hearts of the people who are coming to know him from great darkness. They are practical in that we can now use a beautiful, safe site to minister to people more effectively.

It's a very good thing to ask, 'Why did God originally plant a church in this place?' and to ask that question of our own congregation. Another thing that we were able to look into was the history of Peckham itself, to help us be strategic and effective in our mission. We quickly saw that it's the kind of place where waves of immigration come. Harriet Harman, our local MP, in her acceptance speech as Deputy Leader of the Labour Party, called Peckham a 'window on the world'. We have this incredible privilege – we get to see what's about to happen in waves of immigration, before they hit the rest of the UK. This enables us to do mission with people from countless cultures, and perhaps to have a prophetic edge as a church within our national church – seeing what might be coming next. South London was home to the radical Christ-denying theologies of the 1960s, and a vigorous policy of tearing churches down in 'pastoral reorganisation' – even though, at the same time, South London was filling up with new Christians from outside the UK, many of them from the Caribbean and Africa. We live with the consequences of the Anglo-Saxon heresies and lack of vision, but also we benefit from faith-filled Caribbean and African vibrancy and passion.

London is the city of the Salvation Army; Cambridge was the home of Charles Simeon and the missionary Henry Martyn and the Cambridge seven; Bristol has George Muller; Sheffield, Birmingham, Liverpool, Manchester, Edinburgh and Cardiff all have their stories. Every city and village in the UK has a Christian history that gives context to our present situations.

When in Oxford, a city steeped in history – the evidence of which is in every beautiful building on every street in the city centre – our minds naturally resonated with the martyrs Cranmer, Latimer and Ridley. In St Michael's at the Northgate Church there is a door from the cell where they awaited trial; a stone marks the point of their burning in Broad Street; and near by there is a little room where the Wesleys and Whitfield met with friends for prayer and were first called the Methodists.

We walked in the Meadows of Christchurch where George Whitfield battled in prayer outdoors overnight, longing to be born again, and we lived next to Pembroke College, where he was a student and was converted. In 1860, in a room in the university museum, Samuel Wilberforce and Thomas Huxley battled out the first debate on evolution since Darwin published *The Origin of the Species*. Huxley argued that the biological evidence presented a clear choice between science and belief in the word of God. But 140 years later, we were involved in an evangelistic event in the same room, presenting the inescapable evidence that we have been made for relationship with God. History is important.

Chapter 10

Deeply Immersed (2)

We have an option, then, to be a deeply immersed church, and this is going to involve action. Our worship, our understanding and appreciation of the word, our grasp of and response to history are all significant, and they will lead us to take action. But what might this look like? Evangelicals are stereotypically activists, but we believe that this can be a deep, thoughtful, passionate, compassionate, profound and strategic kind of action.

Action

We have three central planks to our action as a deeply immersed church. The first, we call 'total saturation'; the second is 'vision for the year'; the third is 'seasons'.

Total saturation is this: What would it be like if our church, rather than being just a little friendship network, was totally saturated within our community? By which I mean that every person living in our area, within walking distance of our church, would be touched in some way by the ministry of our church and, in particular, would have had an opportunity to hear the gospel and respond to it.

Total saturation

If that is the vision, how do we get there? Total saturation across everything means every age, every background, every ethnic and racial group, the people in the schools, the people in the old-age homes, every socio-economic strata within our community, every government agency, university, council estate, club, shop, pub – every conceivable group would be touched by the ministry of Jesus through All Saints. The police recently did study in our area and said there were 300 distinct cultures and communities represented in Peckham! As we began to try to understand about being more deeply immersed, we thought, 'Gosh, this total saturation vision is even larger than we first thought. We've got our work cut out for us!' In our ministry as a church, we are trying to respond to that. We believe that if God is the God of everything, then total saturation, getting the gospel to everybody, must be what we are called to be involved in. We cannot convert everyone, even if we got the gospel to everybody. Some people would choose to accept the Lord Jesus, others would not. But our part of the deal is to make sure that at least they have the option. That's total saturation – that, if anyone in our community finds themselves in trouble and thinks, however fleetingly, 'I need God', then they know where to come, or they know someone from All Saints who can demonstrate God's love and the gospel to them in that situation.

Vision for the year

The second thing is 'vision for the year'. This is how we are able to be responsive and sensitive to the Holy Spirit as a church and not overly programme orientated. We want to hold together being prayerfully strategic in our action and prophetically responsive in the moment, and in the year as a whole. We believe that every church member can hear from the Lord, and so we have often experienced many congregation members ringing or emailing in Bible verses, words and pictures which confirm what the Lord is showing us for the year ahead. At the start of each year, after a process of listening, I (Frog) preach a sermon setting out this vision as best I can. I got the idea for this from watching another church leader, Mike Breen, in action in Sheffield whilst I was training for ordination, and I was inspired to do the same by discovering that the original vicar of All Saints had also done this every year. We increasingly feel this is a helpful discipline, and have almost invariably seen these visions unfolding across the year.

Seasons

Growing the life of a church as well as immersing ourselves with mission passion in our community can be daunting, so a sense of rhythm is vital for healthy mission and ministry. In many churches this is marked through the celebrations of the church calendar, but a congregation engaged in the community and deeply immersed will be running services, youth and children's activities and groups which demand time, money and energy from a significant proportion of the body of Christ. Times of work and rest are needed for sustainable mission. We cannot do everything all the time, though we might be able to do all that the Lord wants us to do termly, annually or even bi-annually. Therefore we might be called to run a parenting course or a marriage course, but only once or twice a year, whereas the small groups meet weekly. Once a quarter we may host a night of prayer – but not every week. Also certain months are conducive to different types of ministry and mission. January is a good time to think about ministries that might resonate with natural 'new year's resolution' emotions and convictions. In the months of July and August we suspend the small groups and do social and mission activities as a whole church. The social event is called 'Summer Sundays' – all the August morning services are followed by free food for all in the gardens, with some guest musicians.

We have also run a summer mission called 'God Loves Peckham'. We wanted something for everyone in our community, so that no one was missed out, but we put most effort into the young people in our area. We realised that a mission of this size would require partnership and people power, so we started recruiting friends from other churches in England and Ireland, and even friends from the USA. Some wonderful basketball players joined us for a couple of weeks and did free basketball coaching in one of the local clubs. We had free barbeques in our local area, all in the same week. Some Christian football coaches came and did a week of free coaching as well. We had arts and music, and a gospel choir of children from the estates. Our vision was to do it so intensively over a period of a week or two that we would somehow get through to everybody, so that everybody would know that something was going on. We made it clear that it was Jesus who was doing this, and that we were doing it *in* the name of Jesus and *for* Jesus as well.

When we wear the T-shirts that say 'God Loves Peckham', we get stopped in the street by people who say, 'What do you mean, God loves Peckham? He can't – it's a ******* hole!' One of the guys on our team, called Eddie, was stopped in the street by a man outside a pub, who said, 'You've got two minutes – tell me why God loves Peckham and why you're a Christian.' Eddie was expecting just to wear a T-shirt because we were all wearing them, so he hadn't quite prepared himself for that one!

As the seasons come and go, we work and rest as a church with the rhythm of the year.

Mission

Sometimes churches assume that many people in the local area know what they are about, but this is not necessarily the case. Part of our job in mission is trying to create bridge events – opportunities for people to hear the gospel.

We have found it helpful to envisage mission contact in the form of a funnel. If you make initial contact with thousands, deeper contact with hundreds, discipleship with fifties and mentoring leaders with tens, you are dealing in the right proportions for healthy church growth. If you make initial contact only with tens, the outcome of growth will be negligible.

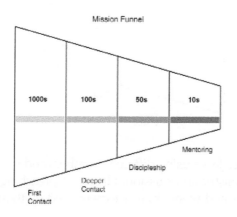

Mission Funnel

A key emphasis for every ministry of our church is that we need to have contact with the thousands to have any hope of building up future leaders from converts in their tens. This is uncomfortable, since mentoring the saved is easier than pioneering in mission. I (Frog) have found it helpful to think of this in terms of colours as well – moving from first contact, through deeper contact, discipleship and mentoring and raising up new leaders. The children's ministry, for example, places a little colour code beside each activity, and at the end of the month we try to take a health-check within the team about what types of contact and relationship we are making. This is where numbers become less or more important. If you have spent a week only working with twelve people, that might be a bad use of your time, unless it's a leaders' team retreat, in which case you are following Jesus' model of leadership development in his handling of relationships and nurture and inspiration with the twelve disciples.

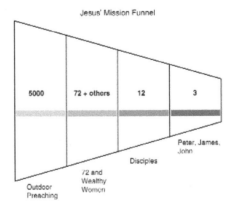

We also see Jesus using different numbers and relationships in His ministry and mission. His street preaching ministry with signs and wonders was experienced by thousands, in both formal and informal settings. He then worked down to smaller numbers in homes and synagogues, but also with larger groups of disciples represented in the sending out of the seventy-two. The seventy-two knew more of the message and ministry than the crowds, and so were key communicators of Jesus' message to other towns and villages. The twelve lived and shared life with Jesus – ate, drank, slept, prayed with Him, watched Him perform miracles, walk on water and raise the dead. The three – Peter, James and John – were given access to closer levels of intimacy and responsibility, even seeing the Transfiguration. Peter failed and had flaws, but this very close intimacy prepared him for a lifetime of fruitful ministry.

Where does conversion fit into this approach to mission? Again, it's easier to show this with a diagram. This process would assume that somewhere along the line a genuine commitment to Jesus Christ has been made, but is not prescriptive as to where or when that should be. A course like Alpha could be seen as sustained contact with those who are self-consciously not part of the church, or else a refresher simply going over the basics for new Christians, and thus a discipleship course.

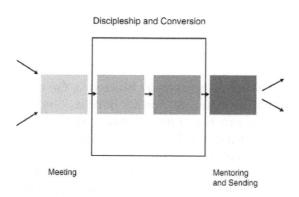

Discipleship and Conversion

Meeting

Mentoring
and Sending

We have developed and used courses at both of these two middle stages, as people explore and grow their spiritual lives from innumerable different backgrounds and cultures.

The reality of church life today is that those who join a church could be at any stage on their spiritual journey, and may also move on at any stage in their maturity. We have to say goodbye to believers who have only followed Christ for a few weeks and help them settle into a new church back home when au-pairs or language students come to Christ. Conversely, people can join at any stage of maturity, and so effort must go into finding their gifts and using them as swiftly as possible, as shown in this picture:

Newcomers and Maturity

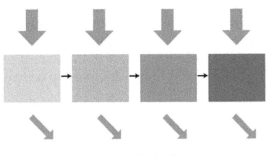

Transfer and Moving On

One area which is necessarily blurred is the concept of membership – there are porous borders, and a looser theology and practice of membership within the congregation than you might find in some other churches. We do have an electoral roll for an annual vote on leaders and church council members, but membership is exercised through involvement and attendance within the congregation. The mystery of the Christian faith is that our essential membership in the body of Christ is not a church institution process, but becomes real by faith, and then may be marked by baptism. We emphasise belonging, and this has led to new members exercising roles within the body in just a few months, if they have demonstrated the gifting, character and enthusiasm of service.

It might be helpful to give a worked example – bearing in mind that we often shift and develop specifics. This is a snapshot of two very different areas of ministry within All Saints, and how we fit our activities into this idea of a mission funnel.

Amy had a dream one night, probably in our first couple of months, of us doing carol singing on the train platform, at dawn as the commuters came in and out, just before Christmas. So we decided to go for it, and for our first Christmas we had a bunch of forty of us singing carols and giving out free tea and coffee to every commuter, along with a little news-sheet containing puzzles, testimonies, interesting facts and a letter from the vicar (me). We now do this every year. In Britain there is a kind of 'folk Christianity' which remains submerged for much of the year, but it can rise to the surface for a week or so every Christmas before the indulgence takes over, and we aim to step in and take the opportunity. We invite people to our carol service and Christmas services, and our attendance tripled in the first year we did this – from about 120 to well over 300 at the carol service. In 2007 nearly 1,000 people attended the various carol services.

In the last two years we have also had a service with children in mind, complete with a live donkey, and this is growing in popularity as well. From here, those interested can keep attending church, or join an Alpha or

Specific Ministries: Commuters

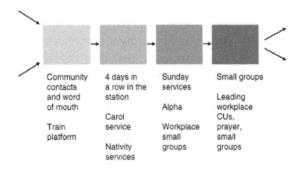

Community contacts and word of mouth	4 days in a row in the station	Sunday services	Small groups
Train platform	Carol service	Alpha	Leading workplace CUs,
	Nativity services	Workplace small groups	prayer, small groups

discipleship course. Many have made that wonderful journey in recent years and have come to the Lord and joined All Saints. Over the four days we have contact with over 8,000 people, and give flyers and invitations into the hands of 5,000.

Taking the model of the mission funnel, we now have regular contact with over 500 children and young people each week in the various clubs, groups and ministries which have been pioneered. We realise, of course, that this type of ministry is going on in countless churches across the country, and that some congregations are experiencing more fruit and blessing in this area than we are. We have been keen to learn as much as we can from what other churches are doing, so we offer this in the same spirit.

At Easter 2006, as I (Frog) was praying and we were beginning to gear up for 'God Loves Peckham' again, I was reading the Gospel passage about the miraculous catch of fish. Jesus tells them to throw their net out, and they catch 153 fish. I had this little moment as I was reading it, and I felt that the Holy Spirit was saying, 'I want you to pray for 153 people to pray prayers of commitment before the end of "God Loves Peckham".'

Now, 'God Loves Peckham' was the first week in August, and I was having this in my quiet time the week before Easter, so I thought, 'My goodness! I don't know if this is the Lord.' But I kind of prayed it over and I thought, 'Well, maybe it is the Lord. Even if it isn't, if we're praying for it, we might see somebody become a Christian, so let's kind of do it!' I remember sharing it with the staff team.

Well, in the three weeks leading up to Easter and the week afterwards, 43 people came to Christ in our kids' clubs. Then we went through May and June, and by July my prayers were starting to change. They were more along the lines of: 'Lord, we pray for 153 people to come to know you by the end of the Summer. . . . Lord, we pray that, by the end of the year, we get 153 people coming to know you.'

But on the first *day* of our mission, 22 people gave their lives to the Lord, and we thought, 'Wow! Something's up here. This is very exciting!' During the course of the 'God Loves Peckham' week in 2006, we had a little taste of something really special – a little taste of heaven.

That summer, on one of the estates it had been getting really tricky. The police had told us that there was a fledgling new gang emerging on this estate within our parish. The police were thrilled that we were going to be there every day doing free barbeques, basketball and football. It was tough going, so one of the people from the team went back to our church hall, where some members were cooking up the goat curry for lunch. He told them, 'We really need to pray.' So Geurline and Nesta put the goat curry to one side and they cried out to God. They had been told that underneath one of the children's slides in the playground of this estate was a bunch of four young people who were dealing drugs and leading children astray. Geurline and Nesta prayed for those young people, and for a breakthrough on the estate. As they were praying, S.o. G. (a.k.a. Craig Allen), one of the American Christian rappers who were working with us, went in underneath this slide. He started talking to them and led four of them to Christ there and then.

By the end of 'God Loves Peckham', 153 people had prayed prayers of commitment since the week before Easter. And the following week at Soul Survivor, another 11 came through. That's the wonderful bit. There is wonder, but no triumphalism, because we haven't managed to pick up every single one of those people. Some have drifted away but others have joined our church or another church.

Leadership

Our final thought is just to encourage you, if you are a community leader in any way, shape or form, to integrate your faith with what you're doing in your community. But also try to encourage your church leader in their calling as a leader in the community. This may involve introducing them to people in the community that you know so that they can get into your circles and make Jesus known there. It may be that you are a school governor, a teacher, a head teacher, a police officer, a social worker, someone working in the National Health Service, a full-time parent, a business person, a caregiver, a lawyer, a bus-driver or a book-keeper. All of us are called to be Christian leaders in our community. As Christians out there in the community, we can live

Christ-like lives which point to him. We can work for justice, mercy and integrity where we are, and we can speak out when we have the opportunity to tell others about him. An astounding fact is that through the church as the body of Christ, the majority of workplaces have a witness to Christ in them – someone like you and I, called to be the priest and leader there.

Chapter 11

Deeply Urban

By F. Orr-Ewing

We want to end this book with what it means to be Deep Church in the city. So many of the world's people live in cities, and Jesus' words over Jerusalem in Luke 13 powerfully challenge us to re-evaluate our Christian perspective on the city. For us, living in inner-city Peckham, this has been utterly essential.

Peckham started out as a small village – it is even mentioned in the *Domesday Book*. It was swallowed up by the rapid expansion of London in the 1850s, when it was a new urban area outside the smog, with views into the city and to St Paul's Cathedral, which still remain. The war dealt Peckham a cruel blow, and along with many of London's industrial areas and transport links, it was bombed. Post-war, it became an area which experienced high levels of immigration, especially from the Caribbean, but along with many inner-city areas across London, by the late 1980s poverty and struggle had become the norm. The local authority summed it up like this: 'By the early 1990s Southwark as a whole was the second most deprived borough in England and Peckham was the most deprived part of Southwark.'[1]

Although our church, All Saints, has had many periods of numerical and spiritual health over the years, the early 1990s were a challenging time spiritually, numerically and financially. The congregation had dwindled right down to about twenty, and the buildings had become semi-derelict. The church hall was under a condemned notice, the gardens were overgrown with brambles eight feet high, amongst broken-down Victorian outside toilets. There were holes in the fence, leading to a car park which had become a popular venue for addicts and drug dealers. By 1996 plans were well under way for the demolition of the whole site, and the replacement of the church buildings with flats. A small committed group of ladies in the church met weekly to pray, worship, dance and have fellowship. Our predecessors, Bob and Jane Hurley, were appointed and quickly joined with the remnant to resist the demolition plans and rebuild the congregation again. They were collectively convinced that God had put them all in Peckham for a reason, and that the youth of Peckham were part of their calling. They were prepared to give sacrificially in terms of time, effort and money to realise this vision. Years of quick growth, mission, enthusiasm and miracles followed: the congregation grew. A staff team and volunteers developed, and work with students and youth began and flourished. We joined a congregation on a journey – with a past and with expectations of a future that God had planned for them. This was a congregation at the heart of a huge, sprawling city. Peckham is a place full of hopes, possibilities and potential, and yet it is also a community tainted with hopelessness and despair.

Peckham suffers from multiple deprivation. The statistics bear this out, including low educational achievement at all stages, high unemployment, low incomes, low birth weights and a lot of long term chronic illness. One major challenge is to prevent young people from becoming victims or perpetrators of crime.[2]

When Luke describes Jesus coming to the city of Jerusalem, he writes:

> In any case, I must keep going today and tomorrow and the next day – for surely no prophet can die outside Jerusalem! O Jerusalem, Jerusalem, you who kill the prophets and stone those sent to you, how often I have longed to gather your children together, as a hen gathers her chicks under her wings, but you were not willing! Look, your house is left to you desolate. I tell you, you will not see me again until you say, 'Blessed is he who comes in the name of the Lord.'
>
> Luke 13:33–35

Approaching the city

This passage from Luke is about a city and her God. Jesus is heading for the city of Jerusalem. A city that resists what is good for her but which God loves even though she rejects him. Jerusalem is an anti-Jesus city but she is loved by a pro-city Jesus. As Jesus approaches the city, he comes with a song and a sigh: 'Oh Jerusalem . . .'

When we approached the city of London, we were met with a different sigh. We spoke to friends about coming to London, and specifically the inner-city bit of it, and many expressed surprised. Some said, 'Why? I didn't know you had a heart for the poor.' Others said, 'Oh, poor you – all that pollution and dirt!' We were struck by the level of surprise and distaste amongst some Christians. So, on making our way to London, we made a conscious decision to think well and speak well of the city we had been called to serve and minister within. The traffic, the pollution, the dirt – these are all realities, but so too are the vibrant people and the can-do attitude, and these quickly became more noticeable than the smoky skies. The anti-city instinct is probably a combination of lifestyle preference and the remnants of Victorian romanticism which somehow linger in our cultural nostrils.

How do we approach the city with a song? One could get the impression, when we look at our Christian hymns and songs, that the city is completely absent from the Bible. Unconsciously we may be building up a romantic yearning and longing for the countryside in our songs:

There is a green hill far away
without a city wall,
where the dear Lord was crucified
and died to save us all. . . .

O Lord my God,
when I in awesome wonder,
consider all the works thy hand hath made. . . .

Hills, rivers, mountains, rain and sun – all of these readily make their way into worship songs. And, of course, it is important to worship the Lord who created the beautiful universe which we inhabit. But the fact that there wasn't a green hill to be seen on the place of Jesus' crucifixion, and that it was the stinking refuse heap of a smouldering landfill site in Jerusalem, so ugly and noxious that it was known as the Skull, has been tastefully edited out of our redeemed imaginations.

We worship the God who intervenes in the real world, making Himself known to real people – including those who live in cities. In Christ, God came to earth in space and time and history and interacted with city life. When we hear the mighty thunder, we are meant to think of the Universe-Maker. But what about the thunder of the planes overhead, or the roar of a crowd? Streets, houses, buildings, community, parties, socialising, swapping stories, work, traffic jams – Jesus interacts with us as we live amongst these realities. Has our worship penetrated into our everyday and vastly urban lives?

Here are two songs with a here-and-now urban grounding:

Open up the doors and let the music play . . .
let the streets resound with singing . . .
songs that bring your hope,
songs that bring your joy,
dancers who dance upon injustice . . .

Martin Smith

I'm going to take it to the streets,
wake up the dead heart while it sleeps,
heaven is open,
come on, it's time to raise our voice . . .

Matt Redman

Though much rap is thoroughly urban, precious little of that style has made it into church and corporate worship on a Sunday. We are growing this area in our church, but it is early days for us. Almost all would agree with us that if there is a reference to the city in our worship, it tends to be the city to come, 'where the streets shine with the glory of the Lamb', rather than the one we walk through to get to work.

Jesus approached Jerusalem with a song and a sigh – we can do the same with our cities.

Approaching the city from the Bible

So how can we healthily and biblically approach 'the city'?

The Bible has a plot-line thick with cities. It starts in Genesis with all the human action taking place in a nuclear family in a garden, but it ends with a city filled with people, in Revelation.

Cities are a place of refuge from the elements – centres of healing in medicine, learning in universities, trading and wealth creation.

Cities are places of sharing in good times and bad – it was in the cities of Egypt that Joseph could organise stockpiles for famine.

It was behind city walls that the vulnerable could be sheltered from warring parties and raiders.

Approaching the city from our human instincts

All that we instinctively yearn for in a city is God's fulfilled purpose in eternity. God's intention for humanity isn't splendid isolation – He is building a church from every tribe and nation and language and tongue – a community for eternity – good and true and full of love. The UN, in its 1996 Habitat Agenda, states that it is aiming for 'just' cities:

> Equitable human settlements are those in which all people, without discrimination of any kind . . . have equal access to housing, infrastructure, health services, adequate food and water, education and open spaces.

This shows us what we are made for, but the UN is powerless to deliver this – it is an aim, an ambition, a Utopia. God, on the other hand, has put that instinct within us, and He has the power to deliver for eternity on His promises. Revelation 22 says:

> there will be a river of life flowing through the main street, trees on the riverbank whose leaves heal the nations . . . no longer any curses heard or spoken – the throne of God and of the Lamb will be in the city, and his servants will serve him. They will see his face and his name will be on their foreheads. There will be no more night. They will not need the light of a lamp or the light of the sun, for the Lord God will give them light. And they will reign for ever and ever.

It is good to know that we are heading to the ideal, instinctive, yearning heart-cry of every home-loving person – this city of God. This is where we are aiming and heading, this is where we will take our neighbours if they come to Jesus. Our families will resettle. We are like homing pigeons with hearts accustomed and designed to be at home in our loft, and at the moment we are released in a faraway land and set to return to the city we were made for.

Approaching the city from the statistics

Cities are important because people are important to God, and cities are where the people are. The Lord tells the prophet Jonah that the plight of Nineveh without repentance is all the greater because of the great size of its population.

The average size of the world's 100 largest cities grew from around 0.2 million in 1800 to 0.7 million in 1900 to 6.2 million in 2000.

Sixteen cities became 'mega-cities' (10 or more million inhabitants) in 2000, comprising 4 per cent of the world's population.

Today, half the world's population lives in urban centres, compared to less than 15 per cent in 1900.

In 2000, more than 900 million urban dwellers lived in slums, representing nearly a third of all urban dwellers worldwide.

Approaching the city from the strategists

Cities work to change society. Tim Keller, a New York church leader, informs us that:

> Historians point out that by AD 300, the urban populations of the Roman Empire were largely Christian, while the countryside was pagan. (Indeed, the word *pagan* originally meant someone from the countryside – its use as a synonym for a non-Christian dates from this era.) The same was true during the first millennium AD in Europe – the cities were Christian, but the broad population across the countryside was pagan. The lesson from both eras is that when cities are Christian, even if the majority of the population is pagan, society is headed on a Christian trajectory. Why? As the city goes, so goes the culture. Cultural trends tend to be generated in the city and flow outward to the rest of society.[3]

If we want to see our nation and society transformed, we need to be Deep Church in our cities.

'O Jerusalem, Jerusalem' – the anti-Jesus city

The second thing we can reflect upon is that the city is not a place for simplistic or naive theology. Jesus' song and sigh carries on: 'O Jerusalem, Jerusalem, you who kill the prophets and stone those sent to you.' Cities in general, and this city specifically, have an anti-Jesus identity and instinct, even as they yearn for a perfect society. In the biblical story, Jerusalem at times represents all that is good in a city, whereas Babylon (or later Rome) comes to represent all despotic, power-mad, abusive, capitalist regimes. We are never allowed to forget, if we read the Bible, the idolatrous, anti-Christ instincts that can bring any city to its basest reactions. The city of Jerusalem which Jesus approaches displays these murderous impulses. This makes the city an intense place to be building the church, a battlefield where Kingdom advances are contested and opposed.

Yet which city of Jerusalem is Jesus talking about? The repetition here allows us a moment to wonder if he might be addressing both cities intermingled, intertwined, interplaying with each other. In effect, as Jesus approaches and sighs and sings a mournful prophetic statement over Jerusalem, He shows His love for the city, but won't let it escape what it would rather hide. He is saying, 'Both cities are here: the one that loves God and the one that hates him. Here is Jerusalem but here is also Babylon – the city of the temple and the killer of prophets; the city of King David and the city of Absolom, his immoral and conniving son!'

Though there are two types of Jerusalem, Jesus says that there is a choice as to which one you live in. You decide which one you live in, by deciding what you make of Him.

The pro-city Jesus

Despite the hanging out of the dirty laundry of Jerusalem, the love that Jesus has for a rebellious and cruel city now becomes even more stark: 'I have longed to gather your children together, as a hen gathers her chicks under her wings, but you were not willing! Look, your house is left to you desolate.' Many people end up wanting to leave a city in search of a better life for their children. And Jesus spoke over that original generation of Jerusalem – they would literally see the destruction of the city and the temple before their fiftieth birthdays. In AD 70 the temple was destroyed and the city was filled with a despair that lasted generations. And this is relevant for us now as well, because too many young people are in need of gathering, in need of affection, and yet are desolate and longing for significance and community. Some go to great lengths to find this in all the wrong places.

Bryony Gordon writes these words about the Welsh town of Bridgend:

Over the past year, Bridgend has been stunned by the suicides of seven of its young people. Yesterday morning every person in the Aroma café was poring over a newspaper, absorbing details of the latest tragedy. 17 yr old Natasha Randall, or Tasha, as she was known, hanged herself in her bedroom a week ago today as her father, Kelvin, and stepmother Katrina busied themselves downstairs. Her smiling face beams out of the pages as she makes a mock gangster gesture with her hands. Behind her, her good friend Liam Clarke does the same. Liam, 20, is also dead. He hanged himself on Boxing Day. One girl said outside the college – 'suicide is just what people do here because there is nothing else to do.' Then there was 17-year-old Katie, hanging around Nolton Arcade during her lunch break from a business course, who told me about a friend's father who had jumped off a bridge last year. 'It's become like a bit of an everyday thing. When the first one happened I was shocked but now it just seems normal, fashionable almost. I don't know. It's that time of the year, isn't it?' How can this be? Why did so many of these youngsters feel so desperate that taking their own lives was the only option?[4]

The journalist leaves the question hanging – no real explanation seems to cut it. No jobs; some drug problems blight this town; but all these explanations echo unconvincingly. One common theme for these suicides seemed to be the desire to make a mark through social networking sites. Those who felt that they lacked significance and community, found what they were looking for in death. The real town left them lonely and insecure, and yet when they died they knew people would post comments on their posthumous bulletin boards, on virtual walls and in virtual books of condolence. Tragically, some people find in a virtual world a significance and a community that escapes them day to day at school, at home and in their streets.

Jesus describes the love of God in a startling way for such city dwellers. He uses an image of a female bird to explain His attitude to the city. This hen will stretch out her wings to care for her pecking and picky inhabitants. Jesus gives the image of loving those who resist you – those little chicks pecking and biting and clawing away under the wings, drawing blood – but the wings stay put, sheltering and gathering and guiding. In the same way, Jesus was about to allow His blood to be drawn by the piercing beaks of those He was coming to save – but they were not willing to feel the embrace and love of the God who made them. It didn't deter Him from the journey; the blood and resistance and pecking didn't divert Him from His self-sacrificial course.

This is a challenge to us as we consider loving the city we live in, as Jesus loved His capital city. He loved the city whilst it was still sinful, fallen and violent. He didn't wait for it to clean up its act before bringing the message and acts of love to its streets and people. He would even weep for the city's women, as He sighed for its children. And likewise, we have to consider a costly love such as this – to be deeply, lovingly urban, as Jesus was in His ministry.

The King in town

I tell you, you will not see me again until you say, 'Blessed is he who comes in the name of the Lord.'

Matthew 23:39

We live in a time of tension in the city, as those who have made our choice as to who is our King. There are a number of responses that we need to make:

- Our *worship* in the city should not be fearful or secretive. There are occasions for public-space worship.
- Tim Keller comments: 'Once in cities, Christians should be a *dynamic counterculture*. It is not enough for Christians to simply live as individuals in the city. They must live as a particular kind of community. Jesus told his disciples that they were "a city on a hill" that showed God's glory to the world (Matt. 5:14–16). Christians are called to be an alternate city within every earthly city, an alternate human culture within every human culture, to show how sex, money, and power can be used in non-destructive ways.'[5]
- '*Regarding sex*, the alternate city avoids secular society's idolization of sex and traditional society's fear of it. It is a community that so loves and cares for its members that chastity makes sense. It teaches its

members to conform their bodily beings to the shape of the gospel – abstinence outside of marriage and fidelity within' (Keller).[6]

- '*Regarding money*, the Christian counterculture encourages a radically generous commitment of time, money, relationships and living space to social justice and the needs of the poor, the immigrant, and the economically and physically weak' (Keller).[7]

- '*Regarding power*, Christian community is visibly committed to power-sharing and relationship-building between races and classes that are alienated outside of the body of Christ. The practical evidence of this will be churches that are increasingly multi-ethnic, both in the congregations at large and in their leadership' (Keller).[8]

- The Kingship of Jesus within the city will also affect our *prayer*. Rather than first seeking politicians or economists to tinker with society and our city, we should go straight to the King in prayer, then back it up with action. We often do it the wrong way around, as Leonard Ravenhill comments: 'We have many organisers, but few agonisers; many players and pay-ers, few pray-ers; many singers, few clingers; lots of pastors, few wrestlers; many fears, few tears; much fashion, little passion; many interferers, few intercessors; many writers, but few fighters.'[9]

- The Kingship of Jesus will affect our *mission* in the city. Early Christianity was surprisingly urban – Paul's strategy involved influencing the nations from the vantage-point of key cities for trading and culture, and building a thriving congregation in those places to resource the outlying areas.

- The Kingship of Jesus in the city will affect our attitude to *settling*. Jeremiah writes a letter to the exiles which is pro-city and deeply urban, but it does not deny the experience of exile and disjointedness: 'Build houses and settle down; plant gardens and eat what they produce. Marry and have sons and daughters; find wives for your sons and give your daughters in marriage, so that they too may have sons and daughters. Increase in number there; do not decrease. Also, seek the peace and prosperity of the city to which I have carried you into exile. Pray to the Lord for it, because if it prospers, you too will prosper' (Jer. 29:5–7). Our city commitment is to be genuine, and not always looking over our shoulders to a possible move to somewhere more comfortable, until God clearly calls us on. Christians settling in a place builds the peace and prosperity of the city they are called to live in. (This is not to denigrate the calling of apostolic leaders who are called to come for a time and then move on elsewhere.)

So this appendix is not meant to suggest in any way that Deep Church aspires only to the urban centres, but rather to correct a mis-tilting of our theological imaginations so that we rightly love the towns and cities we may be living in.

Appendix 1

Sowing and Reaping: The Theology and Practice of Mission

by F. Orr-Ewing

This appendix is a Bible study on the themes of sowing and reaping, as they apply to the task of mission today. It draws on several passages, such as: Mark 4:1f. (the Parable of the Sower); Luke 8:1–15 (the Parable of the Sower); and Matthew 9:37–38 ('the harvest is plentiful but the workers are few').

Although each passage has specific nuances, much can be gained from placing them alongside each other, and drawing on the seed, the sower/farmer, the soil and the seasons. This teaching has been used in training sessions for urban missionaries, ordination candidates and leadership retreats for several years. Feel free to use these simple headings and suggestions to inform your discussion of these passages and your call to mission. The final questions for analysis could provide a basis for beginning a team brainstorm for a local mission strategy.

Earlier in this book we made mention of 'total saturation' as an aim for a mission strategy in a local area – a way to be deeply immersed. This objective is one that is generated from a reading of several scriptures, mainly sermons or parables that Jesus himself gave, and which is borne out by his own approach to mission in the local community as well.

Jesus not only referred to the metaphors of sowing and reaping, but followed these principles in His own mission methodology. Jesus preached liberally and freely amongst crowds, as well as investing closely into the lives of a few individuals with intensive discipleship and teaching. His preaching included strong sowing and reaping metaphors which were not only effective ways of communicating with a rural population, but contain treasures for mission through the ages and in every situation. His mission used words and proclamation, giving a content to the message, but He backed up and illustrated these words with His loving actions, His prophetic actions and with signs and wonders.

The seed

The seed is the gospel proclaimed and preached (the word). The seed is Christ, who can be accepted into the heart by faith (the Word).

When describing acts of kindness, Jesus speaks in terms of 'salt and light' rather than using this Parable of the Sower. Christian experience of urban mission has also shown that whereas acts of kindness are vitally important, as demonstrated by the Parable of the Good Samaritan, the 'seed' is specifically the content of words from and about Jesus Christ.

Another brief observation is that the field hasn't paid for the seed, it receives it. The cost is borne by the farmer, in expectation that the seed being sown into the soil will multiply and more than replace the seed sown.

Mission can be expensive, and a church should expect to invest financially in ensuring that the gospel is being effectively scattered into hearts and lives. The farmer holds back a proportion for the next seed-sowing season, even though he might like to sell it all and enjoy the proceeds. My suggestion is that a local church should decide at the beginning of each year what they intend to spend on mission as a proportion of their total income (50 per cent is not an unreasonable proportion, including a 10 per cent tithe). Perhaps also consider never charging for any mission-related activities laid on by the church – this was a policy we inherited at All Saints, and which has stood us in good stead.

The Sower

In the Parable of the Sower, who is the farmer or the sower of the seed? *The Sower is Christ, generously sowing the seed.*

Those who sow generously will also reap generously – the more preaching of the gospel that happens in our community, the greater can our expectation be that the harvest will also be plentiful in our community. In fact, the Sower is 'good' but looks 'bad'. This parable is almost a joke. Whoever heard of a farmer sowing significant proportions of his or her seed onto paths, rocky patches and thornbushes? A good sower would understand the field, would know which bits to look out for, and could be relied upon to miss the paths and thorns. But Jesus is teaching a theological point of generosity – not always specifically targeting the sowing where you think it might bear fruit.

The Sower is the preacher and sharer of the gospel. Not only is Jesus the Sower, but the preacher of the gospel is also a sower. Sometimes the farmer would employ someone else to sow seed in a field, and we, as Christians, are such workers. Whilst evangelists are often, quite rightly, seen as those who have abilities in harvest, so too the sower is crucial. He or she places the gospel into individual lives until such time as they are ready or willing to accept Christ for themselves.

The Sower is part of a team, and the team grows as harvest time comes. The seasons need different workers. First the ploughman comes, preparing the field, removing stones, getting soil ready for seed. This can be back-breaking work – Elisha was engaged in this before his calling to prophetic ministry. It involves determination, strength and focus – a ploughman who looks back produces a swervy line. The ploughing is friendship, building bridges into our community, perhaps some use of the arts or apologetics in evangelism, clearing the field of huge stones and boulders, and breaking up the clods. Next comes the sower – still the job of only one or two. A few months later the field becomes ready for harvest, and at this point the workforce needs to grow for moments of exertion and teamwork. Harvest time is a time for extra workers to join the farmer's team – perhaps it is their holiday job. With regard to local mission, this is the time of concerted work in a week of mission, perhaps, where extra energy and people power (human resources) may be needed from within the congregation, from volunteers, or perhaps from other ministries or churches, to assist the rhythm of mission within the seasons of a local church.

The ploughman will overtake the reaper. Even though a period of thinking about the seasons of ploughing, sowing, growing and reaping may bring order to church life, and these processes have to happen in order in any single person's spiritual journey, for the life of a whole community, these processes may be occurring simultaneously.

The field

The parable gives us an indication of the field, and says it contains at least four soils. These soils are symbolic of human hearts and minds, and of variable responses to the gospel, from immediate rejection to abundant growth:

- *The Path*: no or little interest in the gospel. These people hear it being preached, but it falls on deaf ears.
- *Rocky Soil*: their initial interest means they spring up with excitement, and perhaps even pray a prayer of commitment, but there is little depth to their faith, and it withers.
- *Thorny Soil*: faith in Jesus springs up and grows for a season. However, the cares of this life, worries about money and other things are like thorns which choke the response to the gospel. At this stage, the process of evangelism and mission seems to be more about failure than success. However, the good soil must also be considered.
- *Good Soil*: this soil is a heart that responds to the gospel, shoots, grows and produces fruit – much fruit. Despite the gloomiest predictions – perhaps that three quarters of the seed falls on poor and unproductive soil – the end harvest more than makes up for it.

In evangelism and mission we cannot be certain what soil we are dealing with while we sow, but only when we see the response in terms of fruit. Even prayers of commitment may occur on rocky or thorny soil, whereas good soil more than makes up for what might be an unusual sowing strategy. It is this conviction which lies behind our instruction to sow generously, and not necessarily second-guess what kind of soil we consider a person or a group to be before we sow – but only afterwards will we discover.

Growth

Seeds grow and reproduce – it is in their nature to do this. The same is true of the gospel, as the word of God. It is in the nature of the gospel, as a seed, to lead to fruit in transformed lives.

Expectation of a low yield leads to a low yield. If you expect a low yield, you are less likely to invest heavily there – but high expectations, and generous sowing, do lead to higher returns. A farmer never sows 100 seeds in an acre, but tens of thousands, and then puts in work, time, fertiliser and water in expectation that his or her labour is not in vain. It's right to expect people to come to Christ, but let's not make the mistake of giving up when we have shared the gospel with tens, rather than with thousands.

Prepared soil is good soil. As we have mentioned earlier, soil can and should be prepared for the sowing process. There are works of preparation of hearts and communities that we can do. We plough, we fertilise, we irrigate, we fight weeds and employ scarecrows to ensure a good harvest from the moment we begin to think about sowing. No farmer can afford to be naïve about the challenges or enter the job unprepared, and so too a local church benefits from good preparation and careful planning of her mission strategy and methods.

God makes it grow. However good we are at what we do in preparation or harvest, it is only God who can make seed grow – the work of the Holy Spirit is the chief agent of mission, not ourselves. And as Mark 4:20 says, God wants us to be praying for a 30-fold, 60-fold or 100-fold multiplication of the seed which we sow.

What is my field?

The ministry of Paul, a missionary church planter, evangelist and apostle, can teach us some specific lessons about church life and mission. In 1 Corinthians 9:10–11 he says, 'We have sown a spiritual seed among you.' He knew that the town and people of Corinth were a field, belonging to God, and that he had been assigned to work in it as a sower. In 1 Corinthians 3:5–9 he points out that the ongoing ministry to them is a question of 'fellow workers' all with different roles – some to plant, some to water, but God making the crop grow.

Questions for application (for personal study or group work)

Self-reflection

Who has sown into me and my church?

Scripture

Read these accounts and descriptions of Paul in Corinth: Mark 4:1ff; Luke 8:1–15; Matthew 9:37–38; 1 Corinthians 3:5–9; 9:10–11. What similarities and differences are there between Paul and Corinth, and my context and task?

Analysis for action

1. What is our seed today? Do I/we have confidence in the gospel and confidence in sharing it effectively?
2. How should we sow? What might this cost?
3. What is/are my assigned field or fields? Are they a local community, an institution like a school or university, a people, a town, an ethnic or language group? Who are my four soils in these fields?
4. Am I expecting growth? How might working in teams and careful planning assist us in mission? Do we know how to harvest and how to lead someone to Christ?

Appendix 2

Deep Church: A Study Guide

This appendix is designed for those using this book with their small group or Bible study group. We hope the guide will provide a framework for drawing on the material contained in the book and applying it to your situation, and we hope it will inspire your devotional lives as a group. To make this easier we will suggest a passage to read or study, some questions for application, a prayer that can be prayed by the whole group, and a song or hymn that can be said or sung together. Please feel free to duplicate these pages.

Introduction

Reading

Please read together Haggai 1:1–9 and Psalm 127.

Questions

1. Do you think the term 'Deep Church' might be a useful one?
2. Have you ever felt disillusioned with church? If so, why? If not, why not?

3. Can you identify four important ways to build a Deep Church in your area?

Song/hymn

Read or sing the hymn, 'The Church's one foundation' by Samuel J. Stone:

The Church's one foundation
is Jesus Christ her Lord;
she is his new creation
by water and the Word.
From heaven he came and sought her
to be his holy bride;
with his own blood he bought her,
and for her life he died.

Elect from every nation,
yet one o'er all the earth;
her charter of salvation,
one Lord, one faith, one birth;
one holy name she blesses,
partakes one holy food,
and to one hope she presses,
with every grace endued.

Though with a scornful wonder
we see her sore oppressed,
by schisms rent asunder,
by heresies distressed,
yet saints their watch are keeping;
their cry goes up, 'How long?'
And soon the night of weeping
shall be the morn of song.

Mid toil and tribulation,
and tumult of her war,
she waits the consummation
of peace forevermore;
till, with the vision glorious,
her longing eyes are blest,
and the great church victorious
shall be the church at rest.

Yet she on earth hath union
with God the Three in One,
and mystic sweet communion
with those whose rest is won.
O happy ones and holy!
Lord, give us grace that we
like them, the meek and lowly,
on high may dwell with thee.

Prayer

Heavenly Father,
may we give careful thought to our ways,
may we go up the mountain of prayer,
to bring down your resources
to build a vibrant church in our community.
Forgive us where we have been more concerned about
    our priorities than yours,
help us learn to become committed to building a faith
 in You
that is deep, bold and long-lasting.
Amen.

Take some time in twos or threes to pray for each other.

Chapter 1: Deep Passion (1)

Reading

Please read together Psalm 66.

Questions

1. When and how did you become a Christian? If you were brought up within a Christian home, was there a point when your faith became a personal, living faith?
2. Have you found that there are any blockages to you entering into sung worship? Are there any steps you can take to help you enter into this more wholeheartedly?
3. How important do you think your feelings towards God are? How can you grow in affection and passion for God?

Song/hymn

Sing or read together the hymn, 'Jesus, the name high over all' by Charles Wesley:

Jesus, the name high over all
In hell, or earth, or sky;
Angels and men before it fall,
And devils fear and fly.

Jesus, the name to sinners dear,
The name to sinners given.
It scatters all their guilty fear,
It turns their hell to heaven.

Jesus the prisoner's fetters breaks,
And bruises Satan's head.

Power into strengthless souls it speaks,
And life into the dead.

Oh, that the world might taste and see
The riches of his grace!
The arms of love that compass me
Would all mankind embrace.

His only righteousness I show,
His saving truth proclaim:
'Tis all my business here below,
To cry, 'Behold the Lamb!'

Happy, if with my latest breath
I may but gasp his name!
Preach him to all, and cry in death,
'Behold! behold the Lamb.'

Prayer

John Wesley's Covenant Prayer:

I am no longer my own but yours.
Put me to what you will,
rank me with whom you will;
put me to doing,
put me to suffering;
let me be employed for you,
or laid aside for you,
exalted for you,
or brought low for you;
let me be full,
let me be empty,
let me have all things,
let me have nothing:

I freely and wholeheartedly yield all things
to your pleasure and disposal.
And now, glorious and blessed God,
Father, Son and Holy Spirit,
you are mine and I am yours.

Take some time to pray for each other in the group.

Chapter 2: Deep Passion (2)

Reading

Please read together Isaiah 50:4–5.

Questions

1. Do you read the Bible devotionally? How do you think you could make this a more regular habit?
2. Do you enjoy listening to preaching? How do you get the most out of what you hear?
3. Can you think of a Christian in history whose passion for Jesus inspires you? Who are they and why do they inspire you?
4. What practical steps can you take to stir up a greater passion for mission in your life and in your church?

Song/hymn

Sing or read the hymn, 'We rest on Thee, our Shield and our Defender' by Edith G. Cherry:

We rest on Thee, our Shield and our Defender!
We go not forth alone against the foe;

Strong in Thy strength, safe in Thy keeping tender,
We rest on Thee, and in Thy Name we go.
Strong in Thy strength, safe in Thy keeping tender,
We rest on Thee, and in Thy Name we go.

Yes, in Thy Name, O Captain of salvation!
In Thy dear Name, all other names above;
Jesus our Righteousness, our sure Foundation,
Our Prince of glory and our King of love.
Jesus our Righteousness, our sure Foundation,
Our Prince of glory and our King of love.

We go in faith, our own great weakness feeling,
And needing more each day Thy grace to know:
Yet from our hearts a song of triumph pealing,
'We rest on Thee, and in Thy Name we go.'
Yet from our hearts a song of triumph pealing,
'We rest on Thee, and in Thy Name we go.'

We rest on Thee, our Shield and our Defender!
Thine is the battle, Thine shall be the praise;
When passing through the gates of pearly splendour,
Victors, we rest with Thee, through endless days.
When passing through the gates of pearly splendour,
Victors, we rest with Thee, through endless days.

Prayer

Thank you, Father for the wonderful gift of your word –
help us to be those who read, hear and act on this word.
Lord, we pray for the leaders of our church,
that you would encourage and inspire them,
particularly in their passion for you and in their preaching.
Help us to be passionate followers of Jesus,
inspired by those who have gone before us and filled with love,

so that we might live lives that are pleasing to you
and take the gospel to our community.
Amen.

Take time to pray for each member of the group.

Chapter 3: Deep Mind (1)

Reading

Please read together Habakkuk 3:17–19.

Questions

1. When you are singing and worshipping in church or
   at home, what are you thinking about?
2. Can you think of a song or hymn that has particularly profound meaning for you because of the context
   you have sung it in?
3. What are the ideas that have taken you captive as a
   Christian which you need to resist?
4. Do you welcome teaching and preaching that challenges the mind? Can you give an example of something that has impacted you?

Song/hymn

Sing or read the song, 'Jesus you are Worthy':

Jesus you are mercy,
Jesus You are justice,
Jesus you are worthy,
That is what You are.

You died alone to save me,
You rose so You could raise me;
You did all this to make me
A chosen child of God.

Worthy is the Lamb that once was slain
To receive all glory, power and praise,
For with Your blood You purchased us for God:
Jesus, You are worthy,
That is what You are.

Perfect sacrifice,
Crushed by God for us,
Bearing in Your hurt all that I deserve.
Misjudged for my misdeeds,
You suffered silently,
The only guiltless man in all of history.

How worthy is the Lamb . . .

Brenton Brown & Don Williams,
© 2005 Thankyou Music

Prayer

Father, we offer you our minds –
help us in our doubts, our failings and struggles –
we want you to be Lord of our minds.
Help us to worship you with our minds
and train us as we read your word and hear Bible
    teaching,
that our minds may be stretched, inspired and renewed.
In Jesus' name.
Amen.

Pray for each other in greater depth.

Chapter 4: Deep Mind (2)

Reading

Please read together Colossians 2:6–8.

Questions

1. Which Christian thinkers have you enjoyed reading in the past? Are there any Christian thinkers you would like to read more of? Why?
2. Do you find it easy to talk to non-Christians about your faith, giving 'reasons' for the hope that you have in Christ? (See 1 Pet. 3:15.)
3. Are there any actions you can take in using your Christian mind in your workplace or family?
4. How can you encourage your church leaders to develop their thinking as Christians?

Song/hymn

Sing or read the song, 'The Power of Your Love':

Lord I come to You
Let my heart be changed, renewed
Flowing from the grace
That I've found in You.

Lord I've come to know
The weaknesses I see in me
Will be stripped away
By the power of Your love.

Hold me close
Let Your love surround me
Bring me near
Draw me to Your side.

And as I wait
I'll rise up like the eagle
And I will soar with You
Your Spirit leads me on
In the power of Your love.

Lord unveil my eyes
Let me see You face to face
The knowledge of Your love
As You live in me.

Lord renew my mind
As Your will unfolds in my life
In living every day
By the power of Your love.

Prayer

By Pandita Ramabai Sarasvati, who came to Christ as a noted female Hindu Sanskrit scholar:

Some wear beads around their neck
Some place the mark of religion on their forehead
But my mind found joy
At the feet of Jesus.

Some make penance going through fire
I abandoned all these falsehoods

But my mind found joy
At the feet of Jesus.

And an Anglican prayer:

Holy God,
faithful and unchanging:
enlarge our minds with the knowledge of your truth,
and draw us more deeply into the mystery of your
    love,
that we may truly worship you,
Father, Son and Holy Spirit,
one God, now and for ever.

Pray for each other about any issues that have been raised personally.

Chapter 5: Deep Character (1)

Reading

Please read together Proverbs 3.

Questions

1. What are the issues of character in our lives which we need the Holy Spirit to put his finger on? Issues of anger, or selfishness, or cowardice, issues of unclean language or thoughts, jealousy, pride, materialism? And what are the virtues, the things that we need to build up in our inner lives – courage, service, generosity, kindness, faithfulness?
2. What does the idea of 'moral worship' mean to you practically?

3. Is there any passage of Scripture which is shaping your character at the moment?
4. Are there any Christians in history or in the present whose Christian character has inspired you?

Song/hymn

Sing or read out the song, 'Majesty (Here I Am)':

Here I am, humbled by your Majesty
Covered by your grace so free
Here I am, knowing I'm a sinful man
Covered by the blood of the Lamb.

Now I've found the greatest love of all is mine
Since you laid down your life
The greatest sacrifice

Majesty, Majesty
Your grace has found me just as I am
Empty handed, but alive in your hands
Majesty, Majesty
Forever I am changed by your love
In the presence of your Majesty

Here I am, humbled by the love that you give
Forgiven so that I can forgive
Here I stand, knowing that I'm your desire
Sanctified by glory and fire

Now I've found the greatest love of all is mine
Since you laid down your life
The greatest sacrifice

Stu Garrard/Martin Smith,
© 2003 Curious? Music UK

Prayer

Saint Francis' appeal to God the Father:

> Almighty, eternal, just, and merciful God, grant us in our
> misery the grace to do for You alone
> What we know You want us to do, and always to desire
> what pleases You.
> Thus, inwardly cleansed, interiorly enlightened, and
> inflamed by the fire of the Holy Spirit,
> May we be able to follow in the footsteps of Your beloved
> Son, our Lord Jesus Christ.
> And, by Your grace alone, may we make our way to You,
> Most High,
> Who live and rule in perfect Trinity and simple Unity,
> And are glorified God all-powerful forever and ever. Amen.

Pray for each other.

Chapter 6: Deep Character (2)

Reading

Please read together Proverbs 31.

Questions

1. What practical actions can we take in our lives to grow in this area of Christian character?
2. Do you know of any situations in which Christian character has helped or hindered mission?
3. How do your attitudes and actions impact the people around you each day in your workplace and/or your home?

4. What characteristics do you think are important in a Christian leader?

Song/hymn

Sing or read together the song, 'Purify My Heart':

Purify my heart
Let me be as gold and precious silver
Purify my heart
Let me be as gold, pure gold

Refiner's Fire
My heart's one desire is to be holy
Set apart for You Lord
I choose to be holy
Set apart for You my master
Ready to do Your will

Purify my heart
Cleanse me from within and make me holy
Purify my heart
Cleanse me from my sin, deep within
Brian Doerkson, © 1997 Mercy/Vineyard Publishing.
All rights reserved. International copyright secured.

Prayer

'Lord, keep us steadfast in thy word' by Martin Luther:

Lord, keep us steadfast in your word;
curb those who by deceit or sword
would wrest the kingdom from your Son
and bring to nothing all he's done.

Lord Jesus Christ, your power make known,
for you are Lord of lords alone;
defend your holy church, that we
may sing your praise eternally.

O Comforter of priceless worth,
grant one mind to your flock on earth;
support us in our final strife,
and lead us out of death to life.

Take some more time to pray for each other in twos or threes.

Chapter 7: Deeply Physical (1)

Reading

Please read together Exodus 15:20 and Ephesians 5:19–20.

Questions

1. How much do you use your body when you are praising and worshipping God?
2. What do you feel when you hear that our bodies are precious to God?
3. Why is it important that our faith is both spiritual and physical?
4. How should a Christian perspective on the body shape our attitude to people around us – especially those who are suffering?

Song/hymn

Sing or read the song, 'Meekness and Majesty':

Meekness and majesty
Manhood and Deity
In perfect harmony
The Man who is God.

Lord of eternity
Dwells in humanity
Kneels in humility
And washes our feet.

O what a mystery
Meekness and majesty
Bow down and worship
For this is your God
This is your God

Father's pure radiance
Perfect in innocence
Yet learns obedience
To death on a cross

Suffering to give us life
Conquering through sacrifice
And as they crucify
Prays: 'Father forgive.'

Wisdom unsearchable
God the invisible
Love indestructible
In frailty appears

Lord of infinity
Stooping so tenderly
Lifts our humanity
To the heights of His throne

Graham Kendrick,
© 1986 Kingsway's Thankyou Music

Prayer

> Lord Jesus Christ,
> Son of God,
> Have mercy on me,
> A sinner.
> Amen.

Take some time to pray for each person in the group.

Chapter 8: Deeply Physical (2)

Reading

Please read together Genesis 2:1–3.

Questions

1. Do you ever engage in spiritual disciplines – either abstinence (stopping something) or engagement (starting something new)? Have you found them helpful in your growth as a Christian?
2. Are there any disciplines you feel inspired to begin?
3. How often do you take time to rest? Do you manage to take one day in seven? If so, how does this work for you? If not, do you believe it could make a difference in your life?

4. Do you ever feel too tired to get involved in mission? What do you think needs to change in your life/priorities?

Song/hymn

Sing or read together the song, 'So fearfully and wonderfully made':

So fearfully and wonderfully made
How could they say there is no God?
Reminded every breath that I take,
It's by Your hand I have been formed.

So what am I going to do with this life You gave me?
What could I do but live for Your praise?

You gave me this breath, and You gave me this strength,
And ev'ry day I'll live to obey You.
With all of my heart, with all of my soul,
Let every breath I'm breathing display You, God.

There's elegance in all You create,
Your grand designs leave us amazed,
The wonders of the way we've been made
Speak of Your power, tell of Your grace.

So what am I going to do with this life You gave me?
What am I going to do with this life?
What am I going to do in these days You've ordained?
What am I going to do with this life?

Matt Redman & Beth Redman,
© 2006 Thankyou Music

Prayer

> Almighty God,
> We thank you for the gift of your holy word.
> May it be a lantern to our feet,
> A light to our paths,
> And a strength to our lives.
> Take us and use us
> To love and serve
> In the power of the Holy Spirit
> And in the name of your Son Jesus Christ our Lord.
> Amen.

Pray for each other.

Chapter 9: Deeply Immersed (1)

Reading

Please read together Philippians 2:15–17; Romans 10:11–15.

Questions

1. Does your community know anything about your church? What do you think they think? Why?
2. Do you feel able to affirm the existence of God in public?
3. Do many people in your community or workplace own a Bible? Might they be interested in receiving one?
4. Which Christians from the past are you inspired by? Why?

Song/hymn

Sing or read the hymn, 'Stand up, stand up for Jesus':

Stand up, stand up for Jesus,
ye soldiers of the cross;
lift high his royal banner,
it must not suffer loss.
From victory unto victory
his army shall he lead,
till every foe is vanquished,
and Christ is Lord indeed.

Stand up, stand up for Jesus,
the trumpet call obey;
forth to the mighty conflict,
in this his glorious day.
Ye that are brave now serve him
against unnumbered foes;
let courage rise with danger,
and strength to strength oppose.

Stand up, stand up for Jesus,
stand in his strength alone;
the arm of flesh will fail you,
ye dare not trust your own.
Put on the gospel armour,
each piece put on with prayer;
where duty calls or danger,
be never wanting there.

Stand up, stand up for Jesus,
the strife will not be long;
this day the noise of battle,
the next the victor's song.

To those who vanquish evil
a crown of life shall be;
they with the King of Glory
shall reign eternally.

Prayer

Lord, let us be alert to you in the silence of our hearts. Let us be host to you in our homes. Let us discern you in our deeds of compassion. Let us welcome you in the guest at our table. Let us receive you in the intimacy of the upper room and finally let us behold you in the glory of your kingdom; through Christ our Lord. Amen.

Evelyn Underhill (1875–1941)

Pray for each other and for the church you belong to.

Chapter 10: Deeply Immersed (2)

Reading

Please read together Acts 2:42–47.

Questions

1. What particularly inspires you about the early church as seen in Acts 2? What particularly challenges you about that church?
2. What actions might you take in the coming weeks personally and as part of your church to be more public as a Christian?
3. What outreach are you involved in already as an individual and as part of a church?

4. In which spheres are you operating as a leader? Does your Christian faith impact this at all? How can you maximise this?

Song/hymn

Sing or read the song, 'Kyrie Eleison (Lord, have mercy)':

Look around you, can you see?
Times are troubled, people grieve.
See the violence, feel the hardness;
all my people, weep with me.

Kyrie eleison, Christe eleison, Kyrie eleison.

Walk among them, I'll go with you.
Reach out to them with my hands.
Suffer with me, and together
we will serve them, help them stand.

Kyrie eleison, Christe eleison, Kyrie eleison.

Forgive us, Father; hear our prayer.
We would walk with you anywhere,
through your suffering, with forgiveness,
take your life into the world.

Kyrie eleison, Christe eleison, Kyrie eleison.

Prayer

> Our Father in heaven,
> hallowed be your name.
> Your Kingdom come,
> your will be done,
> on earth as in heaven.
> Give us today our daily bread.
> Forgive us our sins,
> as we forgive those who sin against us.
> Lead us not into temptation,
> but deliver us from evil.
> For the kingdom, the power and the glory are yours.
> Now and for ever. Amen.

Pray for each other and pray for somebody you are witnessing to.

Notes

Introduction

[1] I. Stackhouse, *The Gospel-Driven Church* (Paternoster, 2004), p. 6.
[2] A. Walker, 'Deep Church as paradosis: on relating scripture and tradition', in A. Walker, L. Bretherton et al. (eds.), *Recovering Our Future* (Paternoster, 2007), p. 3.
[3] C.H. Spurgeon, 'Rubbish', sermon on Neh. 4:10, *Metropolitan Tabernacle Pulpit*, 1874, Vol. XX, p. 77.
[4] D.L. Sayers, *Creed or Chaos* (London: Methuen, 1947), p. 1.
[5] C.H. Spurgeon, 'Revival Promise', *Metropolitan Tabernacle Pulpit*, 1874, Vol. XX, p. 18.

Chapter 1 – Deep Passion (1)

[1] Letter to *The Church Times*, 1952.
[2] Joseph Pierce, *Wisdom and Innocence: A Life of G.K. Chesterton* (Ignatius Press, 1997), p. 100.
[3] March 2007.

Chapter 3 – Deep Mind (1)

[1] Alister McGrath, *Doubt in Perspective* (Leicester: IVP, 2005), p.11.

[2] Tim Keller, 'Reformed Worship in the Global City', in *Worship by the Book* (Zondervan, 2002), p. 193.

[3] James F. White, *A Brief History of Christian Worship* (Nashville: Abingdon, 1993).

[4] Keller, op. cit., p. 198.

[5] *Christianity Magazine* interview by John Buckeridge, March 2007.

[6] John Stott, *The Living Church* (Leicester: IVP, 2007), p. 103.

[7] C.H. Spurgeon, *The Soulwinner* (Pilgrim Publications, 1978), p. 98.

[8] D.M. Lloyd-Jones, *Preaching and Preachers* (Hodder, 1971), p. 97.

[9] 'Lectures on Homiletics' in Clyde Fant, *Worldly Preaching* (New York: Thomas Nelson, 1975), p. 101.

[10] Ian Stackhouse in A. Walker & L. Bretherton (eds.), *Remembering Our Future* (Paternoster, 2007), p. 157.

Chapter 4 – Deep Mind (2)

[1] Alister McGrath, *Introduction to Christian Theology* (Oxford: Blackwell, 1997), p. 70.

[2] Alexander Smellie, *The Religious Affections* (Edinburgh: Banner of Truth Trust, 1994), p. 9.

Chapter 5 – Deep Character (1)

[1] David Wells, *Losing our Virtue* (Leicester: IVP, 1998), p. 97.

[2] J.C. Ryle, *Leaders of the Eighteenth Century* (Edinburgh: Banner of Truth Trust, 1997), p. 13.

[3] Ibid., p. 14.
[4] John Stott, *The Living Church* (Leicester: IVP, 2007).
[5] Alexander Solzhenitsyn, *The Gulag Archipelago*.

Chapter 6 – Deep Character (2)

[1] A.A. Bonar, *Memoir & Remains of R.M. McCheyne* (Edinburgh: Banner of Truth Trust, 1995 reprint of original from 1844), p. 244.

Chapter 8 – Deeply Physical (2)

[1] Ignatius Loyola, *3rd addition and notes to the Spiritual Exercises*, Week 1.
[2] Theo Hobson, *Guardian newspaper*, 9 July 2005.

Chapter 9 – Deeply Immersed (1)

[1] *Courageous Leadership* (Grand Rapids: Zondervan, 2002), p. 166.
[2] These were German soldiers, obeying German laws, which had been agreed and approved by the democratically elected government of Germany. What they were doing was legal. One of the prosecuting lawyers, having heard this argument over and over again, raised his hand up to heaven at one point and said, 'Yes, but is there not a law above our own laws?' This is the moral argument for God's existence.
[3] The Gospel in a Pluralist Society (1989), cited in Weston (ed.), *Leslie Newbigin: A Reader* (London: SPCK, 2006), p. 228.
[4] See Michelle Guinness, *Guinness Spirit* (Hodder & Stoughton, 2000), pp. 30–34, 50.

⁵ R. Hattersley, *Blood and Fire* (Little, Brown and Co., 1999), p. 441.

Appendix 1 – Deeply Urban

¹ http://www.southwark.gov.uk/YourCommunity/ Peckham/thepeckhamstory.html.
² http://www.southwark.gov.uk/YourCommunity/ Peckham/ challengesforpeckham.html.
³ http://www.christianitytoday.com/ct/2006/may/ 1.36.html?start=2.
⁴ *Daily Telegraph*, 24 January 2008, p. 20.
⁵ Tim Keller, http://www.christianitytoday.com/ct/2006/ may/ 1.36.html?start=2.
⁶ Ibid.
⁷ Ibid.
⁸ Ibid.
⁹ Leonard Ravenhill, *Why Revival Tarries* (Bethany House Publishers, 1959), p. 23.

Song Copyrights